Against the Grain. [A novel.]

Charles Thomas Clement James

Against the Grain. [A novel.]
James, Charles Thomas Clement
British Library, Historical Print Editions
British Library
1889].
160 p. ; 8°.
012632.e.25.

The BiblioLife Network

This project was made possible in part by the BiblioLife Network (BLN), a project aimed at addressing some of the huge challenges facing book preservationists around the world. The BLN includes libraries, library networks, archives, subject matter experts, online communities and library service providers. We believe every book ever published should be available as a high-quality print reproduction; printed on- demand anywhere in the world. This insures the ongoing accessibility of the content and helps generate sustainable revenue for the libraries and organizations that work to preserve these important materials.

The following book is in the "public domain" and represents an authentic reproduction of the text as printed by the original publisher. While we have attempted to accurately maintain the integrity of the original work, there are sometimes problems with the original book or micro-film from which the books were digitized. This can result in minor errors in reproduction. Possible imperfections include missing and blurred pages, poor pictures, markings and other reproduction issues beyond our control. Because this work is culturally important, we have made it available as part of our commitment to protecting, preserving, and promoting the world's literature.

GUIDE TO FOLD-OUTS, MAPS and OVERSIZED IMAGES

In an online database, page images do not need to conform to the size restrictions found in a printed book. When converting these images back into a printed bound book, the page sizes are standardized in ways that maintain the detail of the original. For large images, such as fold-out maps, the original page image is split into two or more pages.

Guidelines used to determine the split of oversize pages:

- Some images are split vertically; large images require vertical and horizontal splits.
- For horizontal splits, the content is split left to right.
- For vertical splits, the content is split from top to bottom.
- For both vertical and horizontal splits, the image is processed from top left to bottom right.

Uniform Edition of Novels by "Rita."

Price 2s., Picture Boards; 2s. 6d., Cloth Gilt; 3s. 6d., Half Morocco. (Postage, 4d. each.)

DAME DURDEN.
"'Dame Durden' is a charming conception."—*Morning Post.*
"It would be well indeed if fiction generally could be kept up to this level."—*Academy.*

MY LADY COQUETTE.
"Of great merit, well worked out; a good idea is embodied; the author carries the reader's sympathy with her."—*Athenæum.*

VIVIENNE.
"'Rita' has produced a novel as enthralling as Wilkie Collins' 'Woman in White,' or Miss Braddon's 'Lady Audley's Secret.'"—*Standard.*
"'Vivienne' is intensely dramatic, abounding in incident and sensation."—*Telegraph.*

LIKE DIAN'S KISS.
"A pretty story, remarkable alike for pathos and clever portraiture."—*Times.*

COUNTESS DAPHNE.
"It is written with considerable skill."—*Athenæum.*

FRAGOLETTA.
"The Italian heroine certainly falls into most romantic circumstances—enough in combination to break down a stronger nature than that of the little maiden of the story."—*Athenæum.*

A SINLESS SECRET.
"Simple and pathetic episodes. There is melody in many of the love passages, where the dialogue is sweetly pretty without becoming tame or sickly."—*Academy.*

FAUSTINE.
"'Faustine' is a remarkable work, and will greatly enhance the author's reputation as a writer."—*Court Journal.*

AFTER LONG GRIEF AND PAIN.
"The moral of the story is sound, the dialogue smart and lively, and the style clear and vigorous throughout."—*Daily Telegraph.*

TWO BAD BLUE EYES.
"In the present volume there is a good deal of clever writing, and a percentage of thought in the dialogue."—*Athenæum.*

DARBY AND JOAN.
"In this work the author has excelled her general excellence in power of language and construction of plot, in identity, and general delineation of character. It is a most interesting book."

MY LORD CONCEIT.
"It is both interesting and entertaining."—*Daily Chronicle.*
"Rita has never produced an abler or more readable work."—*Society.*

CORINNA.
"One of Rita's best. 'Corinna' is represented as a marvellous combination of poetry and latent passion."

London:
SPENCER BLACKETT, Successor to J. & R. MAXWELL,

AGAINST THE GRAIN

BY THE SAME AUTHOR.

Crown 8vo, price 1s., postage 2d.

GALLOPING DAYS AT THE DEANERY,
BY
CHARLES T. C. JAMES.

"A well-conceived story, brimming over with vitality and humour. —*Morning Post.*

"The plot is developed admirably, and altogether the reading is well connected, and sure to beguile in a pleasant way an evening hour after a tiresome run with the hounds."—*Irish Sportsman.*

"The love story runs on very unorthodox lines, but is, perhaps, none the less interesting."—*Literary World.*

AGAINST THE GRAIN

BY

CHARLES T. C. JAMES

AUTHOR OF "A ROMANCE OF THE QUEEN'S HOUNDS," "GALLOPING DAYS AT THE DEANERY," ETC.

LONDON

SPENCER BLACKETT

(Successor to J. & R. Maxwell)

MILTON HOUSE, 35, ST. BRIDE STREET, LUDGATE CIRCUS, E.C.

[*All rights reserved*]

Blackett's Select Shilling Novels.

99, DARK STREET. By F. W. ROBINSON.
A WICKED GIRL. By MARY CECIL HAY.
GABRIEL ALLEN, M.P. By G. A. HENTY.
THE ARGONAUTS OF NORTH LIBERTY. By BRET HARTE.
THE ABBEY MURDER. By JOSEPH HATTON.
A MERE CHILD. By L. B. WALFORD.
LOVE UNTIL DEATH. By R. WHELAN BOYLE.
THE QUEEN'S TOKEN. By MRS. CASHEL HOEY.
THE PRETTY SISTER OF JOSE. By F. HODGSON BURNETT.
THE HAUNTED FOUNTAIN. By CATHERINE MACQUOID. [Shortly.
FAVOUR AND FORTUNE. By MINNIE YOUNG. [Shortly.
A RAINY JUNE. By OUIDA.
JOHN NEEDHAM'S DOUBLE. By JOSEPH HATTON.
DON GESUALDO. By OUIDA.
JAMES DAUNTON'S FATE. By DORA RUSSELL.
BETTY'S VISIONS. By RHODA BROUGHTON.
TOPSIDE AND TURVEY. By PERCY FITZGERALD.
BEFOREHAND. By L. T. MEADE.

.* This Series will be exclusively reserved to the works of well-known Authors. Other volumes are in course of preparation, and will be published at short intervals.

LONDON: SPENCER BLACKETT
(Successor to J. & R. Maxwell)
MILTON HOUSE, 35, ST. BRIDE STREET, E.C.
And at all Booksellers' and Bookstalls.

CONTENTS

CHAPTER I.
KISSINGHAM OF KISSINGHAM 7

CHAPTER II.
MATCHING 18

CHAPTER III.
TOUCHES UPON THE COMMON HOUSE SPIDER . . 29

CHAPTER IV.
STILL NOT WHOLLY UNCONNECTED WITH THE INSECT WORLD 36

CHAPTER V
YES OR NO? 44

CHAPTER VI.
IS DECIDEDLY WORTH READING 51

CHAPTER VII.
ASKING PAPA 60

CHAPTER VIII.
"THE WOOING O'T" 70

CHAPTER IX.
TAKES THE UNHEARD-OF LIBERTY OF ACCOMPANYING A HAPPY PAIR UPON THEIR HONEYMOON . . 77

CHAPTER X.
MRS. SAINTLY TRIMS A LITTLE 82

CHAPTER XI.
"THE WEDDING O'T" 89

CHAPTER XII.
MILVERDALE VICARAGE 94

CHAPTER XIII.
SKELETONS 101

CHAPTER XIV.
"FOR THE CAUSE" 111

CHAPTER XV.
MILVERDALE VICARAGE AGAIN 115

CHAPTER XVI.
ON TWO HUNDRED POUNDS A YEAR . . . 121

CHAPTER XVII.
THE LENGTH OF THE TETHER 126

CHAPTER XVIII.
IN MY LADY'S ROOM 133

CHAPTER XIX.
LADY KISSINGHAM RECEIVES A VISITOR . . 140

CHAPTER XX.
FACE TO FACE 145

CHAPTER XXI.
AND LAST 152

AGAINST THE GRAIN

CHAPTER I.

KISSINGHAM OF KISSINGHAM

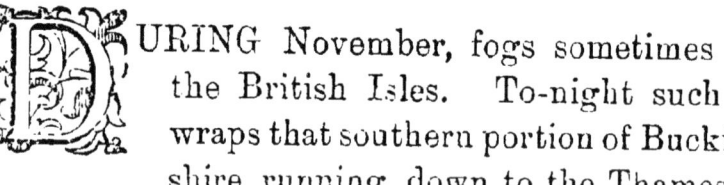URING November, fogs sometimes envelop the British Isles. To-night such vapour wraps that southern portion of Buckinghamshire running down to the Thames, with a gray pall, causing travelling, foot, horse, or otherwise, to be attended with great difficulty and no little danger. Therefore it is only natural that the Reverend Robert Cringleby plods very carefully along a certain footpath leading from his lodgings over the grocer's in Kissingham village towards Kissingham Manor.

The Reverend Robert Cringleby is going to the Manor for more reasons than one. Ostensibly he is going because his squire, Sir George Kissingham, Baronet, J.P., D.L., etc., has invited him to the dinner-party to be held there to-night. The irreverent lay reader may, perhaps, think a dinner such as is probable under mentioned circumstances, quite sufficient reason for a fledgling curate, feeding principally on cycles of mutton-chops, to undertake the dark walk. In a general way it might be; but in this case there is a deeper reason. Mr. Cringleby, as you would observe if it were daylight, is pale, thin, a trifle effeminate, and essentially spiritual. A dreary state of romance has lately taken tangible form and concentrated itself in the person of Agnes Kissingham, the younger of Sir George's two daughters. In plain English, Robert Cringleby, clerk in holy orders, of no expectations, receiving a stipend of £100 a year, paid quarterly, adores Agnes Kissingham with a devotion he feels to be utterly unfathomable.

As we are going to dine with Sir George it is important that we should know something about our host, and therefore, whilst the curate struggles along in the fog with his tender passion and goloshes, we will sketch briefly the career of the Kissingham family.

It is not the least surprising that Sir George Kissingham should be so tremendously proud.

When His Most Gracious Majesty King James the First thought fit, in his profundity, to refresh a fainting treasury by the sale of Baronetcies for the remarkably reasonable figure of £1,000 each, a certain William Kissingham, citizen of London, having made a considerable fortune in the woollen trade, went early into the honours market opened by His Majesty and purchased those four magic letters B-a-r-t. at the regulation price of £250 apiece.

Having obtained (as a business man) a receipt for his money, together with a pedigree of considerably greater length than himself, and a marvel of inventive skill, he searched the home counties diligently for a country seat suitable to his grandeur.

To his own great surprise he one day discovered that there existed a village of the same name as himself, and further that the Manor House and the greater part of the surrounding neighbourhood was for sale.

Here was an opportunity; to become Kissingham of Kissingham had a delicious, William-the-Conqueror sort of sound about it not to be lost. Kissingham became of Kissingham forthwith.

Since that day the family has flourished more or less until the present generation, when, to Sir George's immense annoyance, two girls were the sole result of his marriage. Lady Kissingham died when her eldest child, Elinor, was twelve, and Agnes a year younger.

There were never two sisters less alike than Elinor and Agnes.

The former is all life and "go," riding to hounds straighter than nine women out of ten, loving a horse above everything else in the world, and causing proud, refrigerating Sir George no little anxiety.

Agnes is of that meek, quiet disposition which seems formed by nature for the worship of clerical gentlemen of the curate species.

Elinor cares little or nothing for "the Parish." Agnes spends the greater portion of her life in visiting the poor and ministering to the sick.

We could run on describing the two girls for several pages more, but Mr. Cringleby has reached a small gate at the boundary of the Manor gardens, and has, indeed, come in contact with it in the darkness, painfully. It behoves us to bear him company through the shrubberies and across the wide gravel sweep before the entrance door.

State of an imposing kind, attended by menial marvels of silk, plush, and powder, reigns supreme at the Manor.

The oaken hall, adorned with armour (by courtesy supposed that worn by Kissingham Crusaders, and nearly a hundred years old), looks warm and cheery in an imposing sort of way as the curate, closely attended by a menial marvel who has evident difficulty in concealing his disgust for the reverend gentleman's goloshes, divests himself of them and his overcoat and muffler before the high old fireplace where blazes a mighty fire. In the oak overmantel are carved and illuminated the Kissingham arms—an eagle in full flight, and the motto "Now" below it.

In the early days of the Kissingham settlement in Bucks, this motto carefully sculptured over a stone entrance-gate had given the local wits an opportunity of exercising their powers, and there is current in the village a dread tradition that some daring spirit, armed with a paint-pot, had scaled the dizzy height and added the words "or never" to the legend: but for the truth of this we cannot vouch.

Following the menial marvel, who constantly looks behind him to see that he *is* followed, after the manner of a man in charge of a small dog, Mr. Cringleby is, after traversing a picture gallery (where the Kissingham ancestors are much more scarce than is generally supposed), announced in the drawing-room.

When was a man hopelessly in love ever late in keeping an appointment with the idol he worships? Mr. Cringleby is early.

Sir George and Agnes are the sole occupants of the room.

"I fear you have had an unpleasant walk," says the former, shaking hands.

Sir George Kissingham is a tall, thin man, with a first-Duke-of-Wellington appearance about him which he has been told of, and cultivates carefully. Say Sir George Kissingham is fifty-eight.

"I hope Mrs. Jones is better to-night," is Agnes' greeting, spoken in a soft voice which seems just what one would expect from her gentle face and delicate figure.

"Quite better, thank you—that is, not out of danger yet," replies Robert Cringleby, with agitation. The Baronet has a way of looking at one searchingly as saying, "It doesn't matter what you *say*, I can tell your thoughts," which is very discomposing to nervous persons.

Some people seem perpetually surrounded with a magic circle through which it is impossible to penetrate. Sir George is one of these.

He may have had toothache, headache—perhaps even heart-ache, which is the worst of all—but he shows no sign of such frailty. He might be a mechanical

Baronet (Debrett's Patent) acting by clockwork, for all the humanity you can discover about him.

"The family"—meaning thereby the Kissingham family—is the one thought of his life. The family honour, the family arms, the family name—everything remotely connected with the family, right down to the family vault in Kissingham Church—has an importance in his eyes surpassing aught else.

He has a kind of family conscience by which he gauges his own actions and every one else's.

Debrett and Burke are worthy gentlemen, printing, publishing, and selling volumes containing particulars of the undeniable glory of the Kissingham family and no other. To be sure, there *are* other names in the books, but Sir George looks upon these in the light of those pages at the end of a cheap novel placed there as advertisement padding. That is all.

That the Kissingham family should stand well in the eyes of the world is as important to Sir George as the air he breathes. He is a silent man. Such men are. If the truth must be told, their ideas do not flow with the rapidity necessary to brilliant conversationalists. It is fortunate it is so. Silence, from the days of Solomon, has passed current for wisdom.

The Kissinghams have never distinguished themselves in their respective generations—save by silence. They have never, on the other hand, attained unpleasant notoriety. Their wives they have endured, whatever their weaknesses, rather than brave the scandal of public proceedings. They have ever respected their eldest sons as representing the family in the future, and ignored their other children. They have always lived in great state—too great—and the family fortune has been gradually getting smaller as the family importance has increased.

At the present moment the future pattern to be woven by the mysterious loom of fate is even more uncertain to Sir George than is usual with that profound machine.

But then he feels assured the Kissingham family can only prosper.

There is a quick step outside the room, the door is thrown open with marvellous energy, and Elinor Kissingham comes in dressed in an evening gown of light material, which contrasts in a complimentary way with her dark skin. Women have a knack of selecting complimentary shades and hues—some women. Perhaps a connoisseur would complain that Elinor is too big, too loud, too horsey, for she is none of your *petite* boneless sylphs, all gauze and essence, and more soul than body. No, Elinor is very human flesh and blood, with a strong dash of human frailty about her. Looking at the sparkle of those roguish eyes, noting the fully developed turn of that figure, it is not difficult to believe this.

"I knew you had come, Mr. Cringleby," she exclaims, shaking hands with a grasp sufficient to make the curate wince. "I knew you had come, I saw your goloshes by the hall fire."

"Yes—oh—of course," answers Robert, abstractedly; he remembers indiarubber has a tendency to melt at high temperature, and is hoping his goloshes are not too close to the flaring logs.

Announcement of "The Reverend, Mrs., and Miss Saintly," by a sacerdotal butler.

The Vicar of Kissingham is clean-shaved, delicate in mind and body, and "High."

Mrs. Saintly is stout, and a trifle dogmatic; Daisy, their only child, is the nicest-looking, kindest little girl that ever believed devoutly in stole, chasuble, and wafer-bread.

Mr. Saintly alarmed the good people of the village greatly on his first arrival by instituting a surpliced choir, intonation, and a strict observance of fasts and vigils. This, together with a thread-papery appearance during Lent, told its own tale. Nervous parishioners of "Low" tendencies looked at his new-fangled ways aghast, and believed him a disguised emissary of the Pope of Rome, whereas poor Mr. Saintly is merely an inoffensive, frail-minded old gentleman of the most harmless kind possible to imagine, very seriously afraid of his own wife.

The party being complete, the announcement of dinner follows quickly, and the guests go into the great dining-room with the gallery at the end for musicians, and the carved ceiling, black as night.

Sir George's grandeur necessitating his keeping a pretty steady silence, save when he talks to the Vicar, Elinor does most of the conversation.

"Such a run with —— Harriers to-day!" she says, addressing the company generally. "And no end of people out; lots of falls; a capital day."

"I thought the pack would run through the village; I observed them tending in that direction once," says the Vicar, drinking hot soup with a relish.

"I believe *you* would always keep in front if you went with us. You like to lead," continues Elinor.

Mr. Saintly has no idea of "chaff."

"Anything I take up, I like to carry through to the utmost of my poor powers," he answers, seriously.

Cringleby catches Agnes's eye and blushes.

"I fear we shall have a Board School in the village unless the parishioners subscribe more liberally to our present ones," hazards Mrs. Saintly. Her one idea of a priest's duty is the getting in of subscriptions; object immaterial.

"I should not approve of a Board," says the Baronet, in a tone implying that the question is settled thereby.

"You see, things progress—they *will* progress," Mrs. Saintly opines, sadly.

"The misfortune of the age is progression. Are we, as a nation, what we were a hundred years ago? I fear we are not—through what is called 'progress.' I like to stand still," says Sir George, with a monarch-of-all-I-survey manner. "Stand still and look about me."

"Certainly; stand still, and revive old customs which are thought obsolete, but are really the safeguards of a nation," puts in Mr. Saintly, thinking of vestments.

"There is none of the old liberality in these days," says his wife. "Without money what can the Church hope to do? Nothing. What will it do? Nothing. It's really a very sad state of things."

"I believe hunting has improved; faster hounds and horses; better going; everything connected with it." Elinor cannot leave her pet subject alone.

"I fear there is not the old respect for those worthy of it. A levelling process is going on, I observe. The every-day labourer evinces an objection to touch his hat in these degenerate days—a bad sign," Sir George says.

"I don't care about hat-touching, if he opens gates willingly for one, and he always does so for me," laughs Elinor. "I'm a Radical, I tell you plainly I am. Your old aristocracy has played its cards so badly, it has lost the game—that's about what it comes to."

"Really, Elinor!" protests the Baronet, "really! I regret extremely to hear a Kissingham express such sentiments. They are unbecoming to the family."

"I'm sorry; but I can't help it. What do you say, Mrs. Saintly?"

Mrs. Saintly thinks that "if the aristocracy had subscribed more liberally in the past, perhaps—even if they would do so to a greater extent in the present—there is hope—still hope."

This opinion is reassuring, and ushers in dessert pleasantly.

Mr. Cringleby eats his dinner in a love-lorn

silence, glancing stealthily from time to time at his idol, thinking vaguely the while of the Queen of Sheba. There seems somehow a strange connection, to him, between that deceased lady and Agnes Kissingham. What a strange thing love is!

It is rather a dreary dinner-party on the whole. I think we have had enough of it. We can imagine the remainder of the evening.

Mild music in the drawing-room. The Vicar regretting the state of England with Sir George; Mrs. Saintly discussing parish work with her daughter and Agnes; Cringleby feebly joining, and eventually going home in the fog to his lodgings over the grocer's, having spoken some dozen words to his goddess, and being rapturous thereat.

There are hundreds of such dinners given every night in the country; imposing ceremonies of a funereal character.

CHAPTER II.

MATCHING.

LADY NETHERBY is a marvel of "make-up" skill dwelling on Carlton House Terrace. Lady Netherby is a widow (always dying to be an interesting one) without family.

Beginning at the topmost curl of her false hair, and travelling downwards past her false eyebrows, false colour, false teeth, and false figure, to the ground upon which she walks with a false, mincing gait, Lady Netherby is a dreary, elderly human lie.

Her falsity reaches to her manner and her thoughts. She has aped opinions and concealed her own through a life of some fifty odd years, until now she is often at a loss to know what *are* her real thoughts, which the real, and which the sham Lady Netherby.

Through all this complication of identity there runs ever one firm and unshakable faith—that she is young, beautiful, and lovable.

People look upon this strange belief of hers as a harmless senility, and for the most part humour it;

the world will humour a great deal of eccentricity at thirty thousand a year. This is about the extent to which report will tolerate it in Lady Netherby.

Certainly her husband left her everything, and of course he was rich. Did he not keep racehorses? And had not the Netherbys for generations held the important and remunerative perpetual pension going with the exalted office of Hereditary Grand *Bon-bon* Puller of England? Finally, does, or does not, Lady Netherby live on Carlton House Terrace?

This settles it absolutely.

Now her ladyship had proved so vastly too much for her husband that the peer departed this chequered life within two years of his wedlock, and leaving no representative, the title became extinct. Through her widowhood onward to the present time impecunious fish have nibbled at the titled bait; but with all her falseness Lady Netherby is cunning. Unless she can get hold of a suitable partner for the matrimonial game there is no play in her. Once, in remote ages, a tradition told over teacups says, she really *was* in love with a penniless but handsome suitor. Yet she finally refused him! Inscrutable are thy ways, oh Woman!

At the present moment Lady Netherby is in a delicate-hued, girlish little boudoir drinking tea, to each cup of which she adds a flavouring from a cut-glass bottle containing a straw-coloured fluid. Like all bashful, blushing young things, she is liable to become hysterical and stupid if she does not keep herself up to what she graphically describes as "concert pitch," this necessary tuning being invariably performed by means of the cut-glass bottle and the straw-coloured fluid—a performance requiring great care on the part of the tuner, as otherwise, instead of improving the tone, it is liable to produce

"The little rift within the lute
That by-and-by will make the music mute."

To-day, my lady is very girlish and stupid and out of sorts, the cause being a certain letter she has received from her bankers which annoys her exceedingly—all business communications do.

She has taken her third cup of tea and is feeling the better for it, when a gorgeous footman, yards long, opens the hand-painted door softly, and announces:

"Mrs. Bingham."

My lady jumps up with a little startled exclamation, and throws herself into the arms of her friend, but judiciously, and not in a way to damage aught youthful and artistic about her.

"My dearest Bessie! I've been absolutely dying to see you all day," she says.

"I told you I would call, Lizzie, and here I am, you see; and please give me a cup of tea, there's a dear," answers Mrs. Bingham—a stout, jovial matron, something younger than her ladyship.

Mrs. Bingham is, on the whole, one of the best-hearted people in creation; but she has one weakness, one peculiarity: there is no more persevering and inveterate match-maker in all London.

She may be looked upon as an accessory before the fact to more matrimonial murders than it is possible to enumerate.

Don't ask why. Nobody knows, not even she herself.

She gains nothing by it. She has no daughters of her own. She is very wealthy, and therefore the unkind suggestion that has been made in certain quarters that she "gets a commission on her work" may be dismissed at once. It is a strange form of monomania which, we are inclined to believe, attacks stout, matronly, middle-aged ladies occasionally. If this hazarded theory is correct, such women should certainly be classed as *dangerous* lunatics.

Youthful Lady Netherby, by a deft turn of a white arm that is a trifle bony, places the cut-glass bottle out of sight beneath the folds of some fancy work she is playing with, and pours out tea for her friend.

"Now, Liz, my dear, why do you think I've come to-day—what for?"

"I hope, to see *me*," replies her ladyship, with a pout that is a bit ghastly.

"That, of course; but for something else—something *very important indeed!*"

"Don't bother me with guessing, dear; I've a headache. What is it?"

"I want you to dine with us to-night. Are you engaged? I do hope not. You *must* come. I've got a sweetheart for you—awfully handsome, and tremendously rich."

"Oh, really, Bessie, how shocking you are!" simpers the coy beauty. "Who is it?"

"Sir George Kissingham, of Kissingham; and he's dying, positively *dying*, my dear, for an introduction."

"How is it he's in London in the hunting season?" asks Lady Netherby, with a languid interest.

"Well, he has come up to—to meet young Lord Maidenhair—a friend of mine, you know. For some reason he wishes to make his acquaintance, and therefore, knowing him a friend of mine, he has asked me to do it. They met, and were introduced at Henry's club last night. To-day Sir George dines with *us*, and, as I've said, he's now dying to see you."

"Why will people be so silly?" asks her ladyship. "I'm sure there's nothing so *very* charming about me —is there, dear?"

"Why, you silly thing, of course there is—to men. They're all alike with you."

Even girlish, silly things have an eye to the "main chance" sometimes.

"Is Sir George really very rich—are you *sure* of it?" asks Lady Netherby, with a little more interest than she has hitherto exhibited.

"My dear, rolling, positively *rolling* in money. Noted for his wealth all over Buckinghamshire," answers Mrs. Bingham. It is her stock reply to all questions as to the other person of any pair she is bent upon wedding together. Only half an hour previously she was assuring Sir George that Lady Netherby was the richest woman in London (bar the Baroness Burdett-Coutts, say), and telling him that "though Lizzie was old and stupid, money was, after all, the great thing in these days." It was only after great persuasion that the Baronet could be prevailed upon to come to dinner to meet her ladyship—not, indeed, till Mrs. Bingham said: "If you *do* feel inclined to go in for money, here's your chance ready. She is, I know as a fact, positively *dying*, Sir George, positively *dying* to make your acquaintance."

"So we *shall* see you at night, dearest," says truthful Bessie, kissing her friend again before parting, and after having refreshed herself with several cups of tea; "and you won't on any account disappoint us—think of poor Sir George's state of mind if you do."

And Lizzie, all fluttered and bashful, says she will certainly come—and means it. Dear, captivating, artless little thing!

Mrs. Bingham's house, hard by Hamilton Place, though spoken of irreverently as "the Matcheries" (its mistress being known as the "Matcher"), is comfortably luxurious.

Half the married people in the best set met their destiny and doom in that white-fronted abode. To dine at the Binghams' with a marriageable maiden is tantamount to publishing your engagement in the *Post*.

In the enormous drawing-room there are little dimly-lighted nooks like shrines, screened by curtains, each shrine having had at least a dozen worshippers at it before now, the worship invariably being conducted in pairs.

In the back drawing-room, Cupid, fully armed, has a delicate pink hue thrown upon him by the ruby lamp-shades, blushing, perhaps, at having been obliged to play gooseberry so often, though that is his necessary fate, and he should be used to it by this time.

The Bingham dinners are not particularly good, for some reason. It may be that the hostess thinks good viands wasted before the lovers who usually assemble around her board. *They* would eat oysters with the shell on, in blissful oblivion, for the most part.

"We are only expecting *her*," says Mrs. Bingham to Sir George where they are awaiting the arrival of youth and beauty. "You must forget her looks, and think of her money."

Sir George bows courteously. He dislikes it all exceedingly, but there exist circumstances which would make the acquisition of some money of great service to the Kissingham family just now, and in the cause of the family the Baronet is ready for martyrdom any day.

Henry Bingham has amassed a large fortune in connection with a newspaper of extremely Radical tendencies, and turned a Tory in an old age which gives him small pleasure save geology, about which he is supposed to be an authority.

His wife takes no count of him in her domestic arrangements, beyond having a place laid for him at table. She leaves him, she says, to his pursuits, which is kindly in her.

If the truth must be told, there is no fluttering of Sir George's heart when Lady Netherby is announced; nor when she comes in, with a blush of expectation, beautifully executed, upon her cheeks; nor when he is introduced to her, and she simpers that she was fearing she was late, only she knew darling Bessie would forgive her, and that dear Mr. Bingham never scolds —can't really do it if he wants to, you know.

Dear Mr. Bingham mutters to his wife: "I can't think how you can stand her; she makes *me* ill!"

And Bessie replies in the same tone:

"Do be quiet, Henry. Don't you see it's a case?"

A case it seems likely to be. Her youthful ladyship laughs, and whispers, and ogles the poor old Baronet to a degree long past imagination or depicting.

Throughout dinner she appeals to him, and moves her head so bewitchingly to catch a glance of him round the *épergne* in the centre of the table, that the yards-long footman standing in rear of Mr. Bingham, catches suppressed and condemnatory exclamations evolved by that geologic gentleman, and telegraphs a something done with the eye to the butler standing a little distance off.

When the ladies go upstairs (dearest Lizzie having let her handkerchief drop for Sir George to pick up), Mr. Bingham finds himself upon the point of saying disparaging things of his fair guest, but just remembering in time what his wife had said whilst they were dressing for dinner, "Don't set him against her, Henry, it will be *such* a funny marriage—I *do* want to see it," he stops himself, and merely asks a question relative to the geologic formation of Southern Bucks.

"My dear sir," says the Baronet, who between

irresolution, and the toils of the fowler, is fast becoming irritable. "My dear sir, I regret extremely to confess that I know nothing whatever, absolutely nothing of the geologic features of Southern Bucks. I regret it—for your sake I regret it—but I cannot help it."

Poor Bingham has only one other subject about which he can talk — literature. After a pause he tries it.

"Some very clever fiction has been written lately," he hazards.

Unfortunate!

"I never read fiction, Mr. Bingham. I dare say it *is* clever, as you say so. It is, alas! a clever age—we suffer from a plethora of genius. Every other man you meet is a genius. It will prove the ruin of the country, sir, depend upon it."

"Cheap literature—" continues the host, but he is not destined to finish his sentence; it is a sore subject with his guest, who breaks in:

"Cheap literature, sir, I detest and abhor, and I shall never rest content till it is done away with."

Mr. Bingham thinks it will be a long time before Sir George rests, on these terms, but merely suggests a move to the drawing-room.

Arrived there, Lady Netherby takes possession of the Baronet at once, Mr. Bingham the same with an easy-chair in which he shortly dozes, whilst dear Bessie, who can struggle through some simple dance music, plays polkas and valses which appear like the Laureate's brook in the matter of going on for ever —even though they run dry all the time.

"Tell me all about Windsor," says the gauzy siren, with an essence-wafting sweep of her fan, when she and Sir George are seated upon one of the numerous couches. "Tell me about Windsor—*all* about it, you know."

"Really—it is a large subject—I scarcely know how to obey your commands."

"But of course it's *romantic?* With towers, and turrets, and cloisters, and ivy, and all that—I haven't seen it since I was a child."

"Yes, there are turrets—and—cloisters—and a great deal of ivy—" replies poor Sir George, feeling as one might if suddenly called upon to tell any one, say, "all about Human Nature."

"The neighbourhood, I'm certain, is charming," says the siren.

"The fact is—it *is* rather pleasant—in summer time."

"Oh! and then there's St. George's Chapel—I forgot that—with stained glass—I love stained glass—of course there *is* stained glass?"

The Baronet is obliged to admit the kaleidoscopic impeachment; but he is in no way gushing! In fact, he is only describable in the ladies' graphic expression, "heavy in hand."

When Bessie, from sheer exhaustion, is compelled to abandon her playing, Lady Netherby has not made the progress she could wish with her new acquisition. But she makes a daring plunge as she is going away:

"Sir George" [oh! how coyly!], "Bessie—that is Mrs. Bingham, you know—is lunching with me the day after to-morrow. It's dreadfully shocking of me, I know—but would you—that is, if you *care* to—come—with her?" and then, overcome with her own daring, she is obliged to hide her blushes on her friend's ample shoulder.

There is something of resignation in Kissingham's voice as he accepts the invitation. Nevertheless, *he* goes down to the carriage with her—for Mr. Bingham is still asleep, and the dear girl won't have him wakened on any account—and when the high-stepping pair of bays have whirled away the vision of falseness lightly clad, he stands gazing abstractedly at the crescent moon so long that the gorgeous flunkey holding the door thinks he must have taken too much liquor. He comes in presently, however, and smiles a frosty smile when Mrs. Bingham congratulates him on "the impression he has made," and walks away to his hotel, still interested in the moon.

Perhaps her silver chastity—or age—reminds him of the fair Lizzie. Who shall tell a lover's thoughts?

CHAPTER III.

TOUCHES UPON THE COMMON HOUSE SPIDER.

"NOW, Tom, we shall certainly be late if we don't jog on pretty quick," says Elinor to the smartest of grooms, belted, booted, and hatted to perfection, as he puts her upon her favourite hunter towards eleven o'clock one soft hunting morning.

Tom Slingsby, who enjoys a gallop every bit as much as his mistress, replies with a smile and a touch of the hat that he thinks they will reach the "Yew Tree"—a little wayside public-house on the verge of Fulmer Common—before the stag is uncarted.

Miss Elinor, who came of age last year, and inherited some two hundred a year thereby—the bequest of an ancient aunt—spends every penny of her money upon the latest dodges in saddlery and riding-habits. This is why she looks so spick-and-span to-day, mounted upon a black—such a black!—equal to anything in the way of water or timber, and not likely to turn his head at the widest "yawner" that ever frightened a cockney.

Tom and his fair charge trot gaily to the meet,

talking a good deal. Elinor often says that Tom is less of a fool, and more to her mind, than any other man she has ever met; there is so much in congenial tastes.

Now it must be admitted that all runs to hounds bear a great family resemblance in feature. There is the thrilling excitement accompanying the wild rush of the first five minutes; the struggle for a good place, and the frantic determination to keep it at all hazards; the stride of the good horse; the field decreasing in numbers at every fence; the smell of the moist earth —we know it all by heart, and revel in it; therefore to-day it is needless to go into detail. Miss Kissingham was at the rendezvous ere yet the hounds were laid on, got a capital start, and, closely followed by Tom Slingsby, rode right up to the tail of the pack throughout the day, which proved a long one, with never a fall. Happy Elinor!

Sir George has been in London a week, and his friendship with that wealthy but somewhat weakminded peer, Lord Maidenhair, has prospered so well that a letter has reached the Manor from its master, intimating that his lordship will return with the Baronet for a week's visit.

Kissingham and Lord Maidenhair's father were chums at college, and therefore there is nothing to bring a smile to the most cynical eye in the fact that he should like a renewal of the friendship with the son. Sir George cannot help having marriageable daughters, any more than he can help the fact that Lord Maidenhair has a large fortune and an unencumbered estate. These things are merely circumstances.

"Now, Aggie, I must just bolt upstairs and scrape the mud off," cries Elinor gaily to her sister, whom she encounters whilst dashing hurriedly through the hall in the December twilight upon her return. "Is the guv'nor back yet?"

"Father is back, and Lord Maidenhair with him; they're smoking in the library at this moment."

"Let them smoke," is Miss Kissingham's curt comment as she flies away upstairs.

Agnes never, by any chance, gets upon a horse; indeed, she is rather afraid of them. She has been with Mrs. Saintly at the village schools best part of the day, and as she passes on now to the morning-room, she is thinking only of registers and attendances.

Later, when Elinor has changed her splashed costume for a dinner-gown, and goes into the drawing-room before dinner, she finds her father there alone, standing with his back to the fire, and deep in thought.

To say Sir George Kissingham looks grave is simply to describe his chronic appearance; to-night his expression is that of profound abstraction combined with a certain sadness—as though he had come to some great sacrificial determination which, though unrepented, is unforgotten.

He looks up as his daughter comes in. She has no great paternal respect.

"You've got home safely?" is her greeting.

"Yes, Elinor, and not alone."

"I hear Maidenhair is here. What's he like?" asks the girl, carelessly.

Sir George, like heaps of other people, has a profound respect for a lord.

"I request that you will speak of and treat Lord Maidenhair with the courtesy to which he is entitled, not only by his rank, but by the fact that his father was my oldest friend," he says, severely.

Elinor, not a bit frightened, may be heard, under her breath, quoting something about a certain "little Tommy dearly loving a lord." Fortunately her father does not catch it, but proceeds augustly:

"You ask me what he is like? I regret to be compelled to confess that, on the whole, he is not quite the sort of man I expected him to be. He evinces a strange infatuation for insect life, more particularly for the common house spider, which, though a harmless little insect, is scarcely, in my opinion, a suitable study for a peer of the realm—the vast realm of Britain."

"Do you mean that he's a bit *weak?*" asks Elinor, in her matter-of-fact way.

"It would be extremely painful to me to have to apply such a term to a peer," says the Baronet, with sad dignity; "but I fear Lord Maidenhair is not mentally so vigorous as could be wished."

"What a game!" exclaims Miss Kissingham. "We'll give him plenty of the common spider; there are some fine specimens in the cellar!"

Before her father can rebuke the tone of levity in which she speaks, the door opens, and Lord Maidenhair himself appears.

He is a small, pale young fellow, with long dark hair, and an apology for a moustache, the latter looking far more like a recent indulgence in chocolate than a hirsute appendage, this appearance being supported by the extreme juvenility of his face and figure. It requires a large possession of faith in Debrett to believe him twenty-five.

"My daughter Elinor," says Sir George, performing the necessary introduction with a sinking heart. He has had certain plans in his worldly old head which seem more impracticable now that the two whom they concern are brought face to face.

Along with his other misfortunes of manner, his lordship is painfully shy of ladies. He merely stammers something incoherent to Elinor, and ranges up beside his host as though feeling safer there.

His alarm is visibly increased when Agnes comes in, and another introduction is necessary.

"Fond of horses?" asks Elinor, when a pause occurs in an erudite address Sir George delivers concerning contemporary politics, in which he expresses dreary misgivings as to the fate of the great realm of which his guest is a peer.

"Very little, Miss Kissingham. Natural history, especially insect life, engages the whole of my attention. It is a deeply interesting pursuit—the smallest insect is a marvellous creation, carefully studied."

"The common house spider, I believe, is especially so," says Elinor, out of pure mischief.

"It is indeed—perhaps the most enthralling of all,"

answers Lord Maidenhair, innocently. "It has even played a great part in history. Robert Bruce, you know——"

"Dinner is served, Sir George," announces the butler here, and so snaps the thread of the guest's interesting remarks.

"I've seen heaps of fools," says Elinor, when the sisters come into the drawing-room together after dinner, having left the men deep in cobwebs brought up by the old port at dessert. "I've seen all sorts and conditions of fools, Aggie; but *this* fool is the biggest of them all. Why, poor little Cringleby is less of an ass than his lordship."

"Mr. Cringleby is an excellent-hearted, well-meaning man," says the younger sister.

"Well, there's no need for you to blush about it if he is," replies Elinor, laughing.

"I'm *not* blushing, Nell; how can you be so silly?"

Yet there *is* a heightened tint, delicate as the dawn of a June morning, upon Aggie's pretty little face all the same.

"I'll tell you what we'll do; we'll judge their respective merits side by side. To-morrow is Mrs. Saintly's afternoon; I'm game for taking his Spidership to the Vicarage—Cringleby is certain to be there—what do you say?"

"Oh! I'll go. I'm not sure that Mr. Cringleby *will* be there, though."

"But *I* am; I'll take care he is there. And how do you think I'll fetch him?"

Of course Aggie has not the faintest shadow of an idea.

"Why, I'll send a note to him to say *you* are going."

Again that June dawn flushes up in Aggie's cheeks, promising a very pleasant summer's day for Robert Cringleby if he would only take heart to get up and enjoy it.

"You're awfully silly—really awfully," is her reply.

Without noticing the words, Elinor goes on again: "I'm getting more dreadfully democratic every day. Fancy his Spidership having a vote in the Lords! I'd ten thousand times sooner see—any one—say Tom Slingsby—there instead of Maidenhair, I would honestly."

"I don't see Tom's special legislative attributes, Nell."

"Well, *I* do. He can ride straight—he did to-day—straighter than any one—no end of pluck—he *is a man*, at any rate. As to his lordship, I'd put a common house spider in his bed, if I could catch one," adds Miss Kissingham, defiantly, "and hope it would bite him."

"We shall have to show him Windsor, I suppose," says Agnes, sadly.

"*You* can, or the guv'nor; *I* shan't. And here they come from their cobwebs."

CHAPTER IV.

STILL NOT WHOLLY UNCONNECTED WITH THE INSECT WORLD.

IT has been told you that the Reverend Robert Cringleby abides at the small grocer's shop in Kissingham village, as generations of fledgling curates, when first trying their oratorical wings, have done before him.

From this latter circumstance, Mrs. Negus has, she avers, great knowledge of curates' ways. By a strange coincidence, not entirely unconnected with the "irony of fate," perhaps, the late (by courtesy "the late," for there is a rumour afloat that the unhappy man bolted soon after wedlock) Mr. Negus was what his widow describes as "something in the same line," having indeed presided over the Ebenezer Chapel in the village. It was not till his death, some three years back, that Mrs. Negus "became Church," as she puts it, and took in curates —to "console herself for the loss of Mr. N.," she tells people.

Above everything else Mrs. Negus takes pride in the fact that she is a lady—or sets up for being one—the process being carried out by occasionally sounding an aspirate in the wrong place and passing the greater part of the day in a dressing-gown—two undeniable qualifications, she imagines.

What if Kissingham gossip declares she has a "soaring soul," and casts admiring glances at the Reverend Robert? She is only forty, and tall and thin, and, above all, yellow-haired. What if such a woman did hope and aspire? Isn't it the nature of *all* women to look up and hope?

The Reverend Robert, albeit he is the most innocent man in creation, does sometimes notice a sweetness in the widow's manner that alarms him vaguely. She has a way of consulting him about his every meal in a winning and seductive way that scares him.

This morning he is scarcely out of his bedroom, and in his sitting-room over the shop, when that delicate tap—in itself almost amounting to a confession—comes at his door.

"Come in," he answers it feebly.

Mrs. Negus comes in accordingly.

"What would you like for breakfast, sir?" she inquires with her best manner. "Eggs or bacon, sir? I was thinking of a little change, sir."

"A little change, Mrs. Negus—oh, certainly, it will do you good."

"Oh, not a change of air—a change of breakfast for you, sir. A mellow kipper, sir, is an excellent thing for the voice, with plenty of butter. You see, I know the requirements of a clergyman."

Mrs. Negus's old dissenting habits are difficult of eradication. The word "Priest," she often confesses, "sticks in her throat."

"Certainly, a kipper—excellent," says poor Cringleby, anxious to get rid of his landlady.

"Yes, sir ; a kipper it shall be. They're beautiful breakfast fish for curates," says the widow, with a tone that implies Vicars should be treated with soles, and Archbishops with salmon, perhaps.

Mrs. Negus has the door in her hand, when the shop-boy from the landing hands her a note "for Mr. Cringleby." She gives it to him and waits whilst he opens it with trembling haste, "in case there should be an answer required." But there *is* no answer required. It is only Elinor's note relating to that day's visit to the Vicarage.

With a beating heart the Reverend Robert eats his kippers. Elinor, then, is on his side in the great game of love he is playing! The thought alone is blissful.

What a romantic world it is, all said and done!

What myriad incense prayers are ever rolling up to the shrine of love round all the world!

If we could only focus and get together all the bashful and despairing lovers, all the hopeful and aspiring, all the crossed and blighted ; those who have dreamed and awakened, succeeded and failed; who *are* dreaming or awaking at this moment, what a strange crowd we should have assembled! From such, what a caste could be selected for Cupid's Benefit Performance—even though *some* instruments in the orchestra should prove a trifle out of tune!

Robert Cringleby finishes his kippers.

It seems a terribly long day to him, waiting till the earliest moment at which he can present himself at the Vicarage.

When the time *does* come, and he finds a stranger with the Kissingham girls, he is at first torn by jealous fears. But the absolute harmlessness of Maidenhair at length dawns even upon *him,* and having also a slight knowledge of, and taste for insects, the two get on together exceedingly.

When it turns out that his lordship and Daisy Saintly have met before in London, and when it is further observed that the peer talks whole sentences to her, Elinor laughs to herself and tells her sister that there is a great future in store for Miss Saintly; and high hopes dawn in the ritual heart of the Vicar. "High" or "Low," "Broad" or "Narrow," there is a strange inclination towards worldly advancement amongst all people.

"I like your curate, he is an estimable man," Maidenhair tells his friends at the Manor that evening. "He has asked me to call upon him to-morrow; he has, it seems, a collection of beetles. I shall certainly go."

"I told you they'd get along together; there is a corresponding absence of intellect in both," laughs Elinor to her sister, when the girls are alone at night.

"*I* like Mr. Cringleby," says Agnes, boldly.

"No need to tell *me* that, dear, it's self-evident. I told his Spidership how you adore the Reverend

Robert. If he were a bit sharper you might hope he'd pass it on to-morrow."

"How uncommonly stupid you are, Nell!"

"Sharp, you mean, dear," answers Miss Kissingham. "Hope your dreams won't keep you awake *quite* all night; ta, ta," and the elder sister passes from Aggie's bedroom to her own.

"Is Mr. Cringleby at home?"

Mr. Cringleby *is* at home, and his lordship is ushered upstairs by Mrs. Negus, the afternoon following the sisters' chat given above.

It is a cosy little sitting-room, that over the shop, embellished with some of the curate's furniture (consisting chiefly of *wall* furniture in the shape of photos of his college, in neat Oxford frames).

The two men shake hands warmly; a strong mutual attachment seems likely to spring up between them, which is greatly enhanced by the production of a bottle of port and some walnuts. Real port; none of your cheap wine, described, even in the glowing catalogue, as "curious," at fifteen shillings the dozen.

As the fire blazes cheerily, and the nuts crack with a crisp, appetising sound, Maidenhair and Cringleby begin to get confidential. They are scarcely more than boys, after all.

Then the nut-shells are thrown upon the fire, making it blaze more cheerily than ever, and the curate's wonderful case of beetles is produced from a cupboard to the accompaniment of the Reverend Robert confessing that he is not altogether favourable to the Ritualistic doctrines of his Vicar—only—he has reasons for wishing to remain in Kissingham.

"I think I know them—what a fine specimen of the *Necrophorus* or Burying Beetle!—I think I know those reasons, Mr. Cringleby," says his lordship, bending his head low over the glass case of spitted creepers.

"You think—you imagine—notice that *Cassida*, I had great difficulty in capturing him—that you know?" stammers the curate.

"Tell me if I am wrong—I may be able to help you—are you not in love with Agnes Kissingham?" asks Maidenhair, still intent upon the beetles.

"I *will* be candid with you. I am not ashamed of it—honest, self-sacrificing love is nothing to be ashamed of—I *do* love Agnes Kissingham," says poor Cringleby. "Do you wonder at it—having seen her and talked to her?" His face, turned beetlewards, is of a hue rivalling that of the ladybird frame surrounding his poisoned specimens.

Maidenhair grasps the curate's hand, forgetting all about the insects in his excitement. "Then we are—for I will be equally candid with you—we are—I was going to say, brothers in misfortune—but I trust we may hope to be actual brothers before long—I love Elinor Kissingham."

They shake hands across the departed beetles warmly.

"I guessed it yesterday," replies Robert, feelingly; "but how do you imagine you can render me the help you spoke of?" he asks. Love is ever a bit selfish.

"I wish you could render me the help I am about to afford you," says his lordship, with some emotion. "I wish you could tell me on the authority of her sister that Elinor was not wholly averse to me."

"You mean—you imply——?" stammers the poor curate, with trembling eagerness.

"I mean that I have it from Elinor herself that you have—as she puts it—'only to go in and win.'"

Cringleby leans his head upon his hands and the table and sighs a long, profound sigh of love; then he rises and takes up his case of beetles with a glance towards the cupboard where they are kept. "I don't think we shall need them further to-day," he says.

He is right; in the now falling twilight the two lovers, each moved by that "touch of nature" which "makes the whole world kin," draw their chairs in front of the blazing fire and talk, with many pauses of blissful reverie, of their respective goddesses.

What a lot of romance there is in the world, all said and done!

It comes out in the course of this gappy conversation that my lord of Maidenhair has a snug little living in his gift down Muddlebury way.

It is only worth some three hundred pounds a year, certainly, but then, as his lordship says, "With love—true, abiding love—what does one care about stipends?"

The present incumbent (no connection whatever with encumbrance), it seems, is seventy-five, and troubled with gout about the heart. Before they part, the next presentation has been promised to Robert Cringleby.

"Now let us think," says the benefactor, standing up before departing. "What do you advise me with regard to Elinor: before I leave the Manor ought I to try my fate, or should I refrain? A week is not a long time to know a person in."

This is strictly true, but nevertheless Cringleby advises "putting it to the touch" before parting. It is a strange fact, reflecting sadly upon human nature, that one's friends always *do* advise one's "putting it to the touch," whether it be the important touch of fifteen paces in the Bois de Boulogne, or the comparatively petty one of popping the question or having a tooth out. There are such hosts of heroes —with *other people's* persons!

It may be honest opinion, or it may be a desire to return the compliment, which makes Maidenhair also warmly entreat his friend to try *his* luck at an early date.

Poor timid brothers, standing shivering upon the shifting sands of the stormy sea of mating! Plunge in and get it over; if you can't swim you can but go to the bottom, and we must all die some day!

CHAPTER V.

YES OR NO?

TO-MORROW Lord Maidenhair goes back to London; to-night Sir George Kissingham requests his eldest daughter to follow him into his especial sanctum, a small apartment commanding excellent views of the offices at the Manor, and which, furnished with a first-Duke-of-Wellington sort of plainness, is not an especially comfortable resort.

"Elinor," says the Baronet, seating himself in his writing-chair, "Elinor, firstly oblige me by sitting anywhere but upon my table. Such a position is unbecoming both a Kissingham and a lady."

"Oh! anything for a quiet life!" cries the lady addressed, who, at her entrance of the room, had at once adopted the obnoxious attitude mentioned. "Anything for a quiet life," and she sits sideways upon one of the three office chairs which adorn the room. "Now?"

"I wish to speak kindly but seriously to you, Elinor," says Sir George, sitting bolt upright in his chair in his best and most imposing Petty Sessions style. "Kindly but seriously, Elinor. I have become cognisant, within the last few days, of the fact that a *great* honour is about to be offered to the Kissingham family. I wish I could impress upon you sufficiently the importance and position of the Kissingham family—a family second to none in lineage and in honour. But I let that for the moment pass."

"Can't you cut it short a bit?" asks the listener, impatiently. "As to the family, I can't find that any member of it has ever *done* anything very great."

"I am sincerely glad that we Kissinghams can boast so clear a record!" says the old man. "I rejoice at it. Only the common people *do things*. The privilege of our order is *not* to do things. We have been, and we *are*. That suffices us. If we wish further to increase our honours, we attain our object by *finesse*. We marry, and are given in marriage. The stepping-stone of such as we, is the most exalted and the most sacred in the world—the altar! We marry, Elinor—and we marry *judiciously*. *We* are not carried away by the common weaknesses of the lower orders. *We* do not marry for *love* and such fanciful absurdities. We may respect—profoundly respect—but we do not *love* in the common acceptation of the term. If we *do* love, it is the family. Never has a Kissingham made a *mésalliance*. Never has a Kissingham had an opportunity for matrimonial advancement but he or she, as the case might be, availed himself or herself of it instantly—for the good of the family. I hope these few remarks I have made, have in some measure prepared you for what I am about to say.

A great matrimonial honour is about to be thrust upon the Kissingham family—the chance of intermarriage with one of the oldest Baronies in England."

"You don't mean to say that you're going to marry old Lady Treefrog — at your age?" asks Elinor, pertly.

"My marriage is not an event entirely outside the pale of probability," says her father, "*some* day. But at present I do not refer to such a contingency. I allude to the fact that to-night, after dinner probably, my friend Lord Maidenhair will ask you to be his wife, Elinor. I imagine I can rely upon your discretion for a suitable reply? Remember that I have no son. The family advancement must be carried on by you."

"You can most surely," replies the girl, with mounting colour. "You can rely upon my refusing Lord Maidenhair in the most absolute and complete way possible to imagine."

"Elinor!" exclaims Sir George in a tone of mingled rage and horror, "you mean to tell me that you will dare—you dare—with myself and the family portraits looking on—that you will *dare* to refuse the offer of intermarriage with a Barony?"

"Will he pop at dinner, as you and the portraits are to look on?" asks the girl, quietly.

"When I speak of myself and the portraits, I use a metaphor," says the Baronet, airily.

"And when I reply to his Spidership, I shall use *no* metaphor, I'll refuse him flat!" cries the girl, whose hot blood is rapidly rising. "What do I care about

Baronies so old that they've got stale, and musty, and *cobwebby* with age? Do you suppose *I'm* going to follow 'the family,' and tie myself to an enlarged specimen of the common house spider? *No*, a thousand times *No*. And why should I?"

"Because," says her father, controlling himself as best he can, "because—I regret to have to say it—because the family position has been kept up at almost too great a price. In fact, because a wealthy marriage of *one* of us is necessary to avert very serious difficulties in the future. Think twice, Elinor, before you throw away this grand opportunity."

The poor old boy is terribly in earnest; his voice has an unwonted tremble in it which is strange to hear.

"And if I do throw it away, what will happen?"

"That I shall be obliged to marry—a lady who has a large fortune," says Sir George, softly.

"*You* marry again—you! Then I tell you once for all, before you bring home some horrid creature to rule here, I'll leave you. Understand me, *I will*. If you've spent too much money on foolish family pride, *I'm* not going to be made the scapegoat of it, one way or another. And as to this Maidenhair, if he were eighteen carat gold, solid throughout, and he begged me on his knees, I wouldn't accept him."

"I have spoken fully and fairly. You must take your own way, Elinor," replies the old man, with a face shadowed very deeply. "I can do no more; it is useless to prolong this interview."

"Quite—utterly," assents his daughter, and with

a sparkle in her eye, and a flush upon her cheek, she leaves the room with something very like a slam of the door.

It is the severest blow Sir George has had for years. Secretly in his cold, worldly old heart, he is extremely proud of his daughter Elinor. That she should thus return all his hopes and aspirations about her is very, very bitter indeed to him. In spite of all, he is not a man to let the world see how hard he is hit. The county people dining at the Manor to-night will only remark afterwards what a courteous, polished old icicle he is.

There is a dash of the hero even in pompous, silly old Sir George Kissingham, Baronet.

He consoles himself when left alone with the thought that this annoyance is only a negative one. "It is not as though she were mad enough to have an affair with some unsuitable man—Cringleby, for instance."

Then, too, the solacing thought occurs that if Maidenhair perseveres, time may work a change in Elinor's ideas and opinions.

But, somewhat, it must be confessed, to Miss Kissingham's surprise, his lordship does *not* propose to-night; the reason being that he cannot get his courage and an opportunity in any way concentric. No sooner do the daring words tremble to his lips than he observes Elinor at the piano singing " Drink, Puppy, Drink," or with Mrs. Saintly talking collections. No sooner is his goddess in the dimly-lighted library searching for a book, or plucking a flower alone in the conservatory opening out of the drawing-room, than his pluck sinks immediately to zero.

So the evening wanes, and the county magnates drive away, and the girls go to bed, without that romantic passion dwelling in the palpitating heart of Maidenhair declaring itself.

It is Elinor's daily custom to go to the stables after breakfast. The stables at the Manor are some little distance from the house, and the way lies through a shrubbery.

Miss Kissingham is making her usual way thither the morning following the dinner-party, dressed in the smartest and most masculine of female costumes, surmounted by a felt hat worn just a trifle on one side, and has just entered the shrubbery mentioned, when she hears a hasty step behind her. Casting back a glance she sees Lord Maidenhair speeding in little flashing patent-leathers to overtake her. She pauses and lets him come up.

"Want to have a look over the stables?" she asks.

"Oh, well, if *you're* going that way," he stammers, "but that wasn't why I came. I am leaving to-day, you know—the carriage is even now, I expect, at the door—and before I go—oh! Miss Kissingham, I can't tell you that I am—that is to say I feel—you know, I'm certain, what I mean. Since I've known you, a new and brighter page has been turned in my life. I'm sure you must know what I mean, that I am——"

"Spoony? Is *that* the word you want?" asks Elinor, looking at him with something of compassion in her face, and a great deal more of amusement.

D

"That *is* it, though not the word I was going to use—and *is* there any hope?"

They are standing still, and poor little Maidenhair keeps moving his feet about nervously till his little patent-leathers become dazzling in the December sunshine.

"I'll tell you once for all, that there isn't the ghost of a shadow of hope, if it's *me* you're spoons on," replies Elinor, keeping back her rising laughter at the troubled little face before her; "and it's *final*—so I hope that ends it for ever. You might have stood a chance with Aggie, perhaps; but *she's* gone, as I told you, upon Cringleby. So altogether, I'm afraid your game is up."

The little man is terribly cut up, and he shows it. "We shall still remain friends, I hope?" he ventures.

"Oh, certainly. Why not? I shan't dislike you for your bad taste in fancying me, and I'm really sorry it's not mutual; but *as* it isn't, we can't 'odds it,' as Tom Slingsby says. Good-bye."

She holds out her hand, and the youthful peer would like to kiss it if he dared, but he only shakes it warmly, and murmuring a feeble farewell, turns back to the house, whilst Miss Kissingham goes on to talk of her various mounts with Tom the groom.

CHAPTER VI.

IS DECIDEDLY WORTH READING.

OF course it behoves a bashful, captivating young thing of fifty odd, to be careful. "Scandal so soon gets abroad, my dear," Lady Netherby, all artful beauty, tells her friend when discussing the propriety of accepting Sir George's invitation to the Manor, in company with the Binghams, who are to spend a week there immediately. Mr. Bingham accepted the invitation readily, and has dreamed of the geologic formation of South Bucks nightly, ever since.

"Of course *we're* only asked because you couldn't go alone, my dear. As to the propriety, why, that's absurd. Sir George has grown-up daughters, not *quite* so old as you are, perhaps, but still sufficiently old to make your visit entirely correct, to say nothing of an old married woman like me."

"One never knows; the world is so hard upon one who is full of life and spirits," finishes her ladyship, with a dentistical simper.

The conversation takes place in my lady's girlish, dainty little boudoir, that somehow always makes the visitor wish vaguely that fair Lizzie were more the age she pretends to be, and more the beauty she pretends to be—anything rather than the ghastly embodied lie she is.

Age, like a host of other necessary evils, if met with a brave, willing spirit, is robbed of half its terrors. It only becomes repulsive and horrible in Lady Netherby, and such as she.

Her gorgeous footmen crack jokes about her in the servants' hall, and her coachman makes wry faces at stray passers-by when she alights from her carriage with the affected, youthful gait that is a trifle rheumatic too.

In due course the Manor invitation is accepted. There is always something pleasant about the idea of Christmastide in a country house, with glad tidings symbolised in holly, and good will toward men (and women) in mistletoe. The very thought of it calls up bright fancies of bright eyes and hearty greetings of those old, old days that perhaps exist only in memory now.

Talking, or rather writing of holly and green deckings brings us to a something occurring on the day (two before Christmas) which saw Lady Netherby and the Matcher deciding to accept Sir George's invitation. That something happened in this way.

Kissingham Church, an ancient one, with a whitewashed ceiling and walls that contrast strangely with the Vicar's Rome-and-water pomps and ceremonies, naturally required decoration. There were pillars to be wreathed, and angels' heads to be chapleted, and the pulpit to be fringed with holly to a degree rendering anything like "action" on the part of the preacher a painful performance.

Now the great scenic artist on these occasions is Agnes Kissingham, and her assistant chances—quite casually, of course—to be the Reverend Robert Cringleby. The church is not very large, and these are the two workers, Mrs. Saintly and the Vicar paying flying visits at long intervals, doing very little, and talking a great deal.

It may be that Maidenhair's intelligence from the seat of war nerved him, it may be that the propinquity of Agnes, with her soft brown eyes and deftly-moving, plump little hands, accomplished it, we cannot say, but suddenly—at the most suitable place in the world, too, the altar—the curate, with a great thump of his heart that makes all but inarticulate his amazing words, seizes one of the little decorative hands and says:

"Miss Kissingham, I *must* tell you—I adore the very ground you walk on—the very gloves you wear—everything remotely connected with you, and I *have* hoped—I have dared to hope——"

Here he breaks down entirely so far as language is concerned, but continues in very intelligible dumb show with the hand he has captured.

Agnes does not take it away from him. No, she doesn't—even with the second commandment staring in her blushing face, and though she knows Robert Cringleby *does* bow down and worship her, body and soul. *He* does not heed it either for the moment. He only says:

"Tell me that I may hope—at ever such a distant day, only let me hope."

She does not speak, but he looks at her, and something he sees written in her face tells him that he may.

"Agnes!"

"Robert!"

So they understand each other, and there are at least two happy people in the world, to-day.

"Why, Aggie, old girl, has he actually got up his courage over the greenery and proposed?" asks Miss Kissingham, with her sharp eyes upon her sister, when the latter arrives at home.

"Oh, don't, Nell, *please* don't," pleads Agnes, all flurried, and with the sunrise flush upon her face again. "Don't speak so loud, father might hear you."

"He'll *have* to hear, I suppose, before very long," says Elinor. "Of course you've accepted dear Robert and his hundred a year—yes, you have, too, I can see it in your face."

"But we're not going to say anything to father for a few days; at any rate—till—till——" and poor little Agnes fairly breaks down, throwing her arms round her sister's neck, and sobbing.

"Why, this is a funny thing — these tears!" exclaims the elder girl. "If you like Robert, what on earth is there to howl about?"

The weeper weeps out one broken word, "Father."

"Never mind about father, I'll tackle him if

necessary—if I'm here, that is—I'm not so sure about that, though. If he goes marrying this horrible old Netherby woman—who is, I firmly believe, coming here for that purpose—I'm off—I've told him so; and you'd better have Robert prepared with a license for emergencies too, that's my advice."

"But, Nell, what *are* you saying? Where *will* you go if you leave home?"

"That's tellings, in the language of the crowd," laughs Elinor, gaily. "But let's talk about Robert. How did he do it? Hope he did it nicely, eh?"

Though Agnes does not quite satisfy her sister's curiosity by the details, they *do* talk of poor, happy, bewitched Cringleby for a long time in the winter twilight by the blazing logs.

My Lady Netherby and the Binghams travel down to Kissingham with no little pomp and circumstance. The host is at the station with his most armorial carriage to meet them.

My lady's luggage is numerous and heavy, containing, amongst other things, a small box or case, devoted solely to the conveyance of those cunning instruments with which she is ever unsuccessfully endeavouring to tamper with the works of the great clock of Time.

My lady is quite girlish and hysterical upon arriving at the Manor, and in ecstasies with everything she sees; but she is soon obliged to go upstairs, where her maid has (as knowing her lady's ways) unpacked the instrument-case *first*. The cut-glass bottle with the straw-coloured contents has not been forgotten.

"Now, Mrs. Bingham, what do you want to marry the guv'nor to the Netherby for?" asks Elinor, catching that lady alone in the course of the week's visit.

"*I* want to marry him to the Netherby, my dear? *I* want it? Why, it's positively the last thing in the world I wish to happen; she's not half good enough for him."

"Well, if you *don't* wish it, you're the best dissembler I've seen yet," replies the girl, brusquely. "Who was she? Debrett only puts her down as 'Daughter of blank Tebbs, Esquire,' which terseness generally means that the one word 'unpresentable' might be used instead."

"It's a most romantic story; not very many people know it. Sir George does, because I told him. I thought, for the sake of you dear girls, I would tell him, as it might prevent his committing himself with her. We shall see."

"But who was she?"

"I'll tell you, my dear, only I can rely upon your secrecy, of course." Elinor makes a gesture of assent. "Netherby, you must know, then, was a—a bit of a fool, and fond of theatrical matters. He dropped into a provincial theatre one evening, at Brighton or Portsmouth or somewhere, saw Liz, as he always called her, fell in love, and married her within a fortnight. Netherby was a great friend of mine; he asked me to help him to get his wife afloat in society. I did to the best of my poor powers. Between his title and my influence we did it. There's the whole story. Poor Netherby was terribly cut up at not having an heir; but he died soon after his marriage, and left Liz everything. At least she *got* everything—he left no will. I hope—I do hope that Sir George won't marry her; I do indeed."

Honest Mrs. Bingham grows quite animated in expressing this hope.

As to my lady herself, as we have said, she is in ecstasies with everything at the Manor. When Miss Kissingham comes down to breakfast one morning in a riding-habit, dear little Liz goes wild over the fit of it. She must, positively must come to the door and see the start. Oh, what a perfect horse Elinor's is! What a love; and what a handsome groom she has! Lady Netherby is especially interested in Tom Slingsby, asking his name and even his age, and where he came from; all details connected with horses and their grooms, she avers, are *so* interesting to her!

She appears really fond of horses, and is often tripping, with the youthful but a trifle rheumatic gait, down to the stables, to the great surprise of Mrs. Bingham, who had no idea that Liz could really care for anything but admiration—of which she certainly gets very little.

Mrs. Saintly (who is spitefully disposed in consequence of her ladyship declining to subscribe to some deserving local charity) says *she* thinks it most unbecoming a lady to go near stables, and further is scandalised by the fact that she has twice seen the youthful visitor talking to one of the stablemen, who, it seems, chanced to be Tom Slingsby.

Elinor only laughs at this story, and says that anybody, of any age, might like to talk to Tom, he's so smart and clever.

So he is. Better dressed and better mannered than a great number of men who pass muster in smart drawing-rooms as gentlemen. Sir George often prides himself on this fact. It is, he thinks, as it should be with a Kissingham groom.

It is not an entirely blissful time to Sir George, this visit of Lady Netherby and the Binghams. He goes about with an undefinable sensation that he is selling himself into bondage for a consideration the value of which he does not exactly know.

It is no trouble to entertain Mr. Bingham. Armed with a hammer, that harmless old gentleman goes tapping about like an antique woodpecker engaged upon extremely hollow beech-trees, and with less tangible results than the mentioned bird.

But to the great relief of most people concerned, the visit comes to an end at last, by which time the poor old Baronet has been smiled at dentistically, ogled belladonnacally, and blushed at rougically to a degree past all belief and comprehension.

And yet he has not actually proposed. He is doubtful, exactly as a bather might be, who, standing beside the river late in autumn, and having taken his coat off, is still pausing undecided whether or no the water be too cold; in such circumstances it only requires a ray of sunshine, or a cold breeze, to settle the matter finally.

In spite of this, my Lady Netherby (who never sticks at the truth) tells Mrs. Bingham in confidence before they go away, that it is all settled, and that she will soon reign at the Manor. A nice little lie, which Mrs. Bingham (also swearing to secrecy) communicates, with intense expressions of sorrow, to Elinor before leaving.

"I've expected he'd make a fool of himself for some time," is his daughter's unsurprised comment.

So the most armorial carriage is put in requisition again, and the Binghams, with their lovely charge, are steamed away with from Kissingham Station, together with the luggage and the instruments.

Nor is the cut-glass bottle forgotten.

CHAPTER VII.

ASKING PAPA.

THE Reverend Robert Cringleby has screwed up his courage. He has. With the greatest difficulty, 'tis true; but what does that matter, as the desired end is attained? What boots it whether the bright eyes of Agnes, or the nourishment derived from cycles of mutton-chops, has effected it? What boots it if it be a combination of both these incentives? We trow, nothing.

Pure love for a pure woman elevates the fortunate possessor of it as near Heaven as the impure love for a frail one lowers the unhappy man right down to the gates of Hell—and through them, perhaps.

Cringleby has gone about preaching better and praying better, a better member of society in every way, since knowing that Agnes, his dear, blushing, coy little Agnes, returns his honest love.

Even Mrs. Negus has noticed a strange change in him, and guessed something of the cause, and bridled and smiled, and hinted all sorts of sarcastic things to the limit of what she dares in consequence.

Last of all in the subtle alteration in his nature has come the courage to ask Sir George Kissingham for his daughter. Agnes knows that he is going to do it. Yes, to-day, that following the departure of the Manor guests, she will learn her fate. She goes about in sad trepidation, poor little girl, and there is nothing to laugh at in the fact.

Cringleby, with his heart beating quite a succession of postman's knocks, asks for the Baronet at the great front-door, and is shown into the empty library.

Sir George does not come immediately. The reason is that just before the curate's ring at the front-door, Elinor has tapped at the door of her father's study, and gone in. She is not a beater about the bush.

"Father, I wish to know whether you are going to make a fool of yourself with that horrible old woman, who has a most terrible kick in her gallop —Lady Netherby?"

"Elinor, a kick in her gallop! Make a fool of myself! I am surprised at such language from a Kissingham and a daughter."

"And I'm pretty well surprised at your recent conduct, and I'll just hint that you haven't answered my question," says Elinor, with that hot temper of hers rising, as it always does at Sir George's cool pomposity.

"Then once for all I refuse to satisfy idle curiosity," he says, getting angry too, in a quiet way. "When arrangements have been completed you will doubtless be informed what they are; till then, kindly refrain from importuning me impertinently."

"Impertinence—absurd! Do you think I'm quietly going to stand by and see you make a laughing-stock of yourself?"

"You can pursue whatever course you think best, Elinor. I shall satisfy no curiosity at present."

"Which means that you *are* going to marry this walking sham, and I tell you plainly I think you're an old fool." With which undutiful remark Miss Kissingham bangs out of the room.

She has scarcely left it when a menial marvel announces that Mr. Cringleby is in the library.

"I'll go there in a few moments," is Sir George's reply, given with a face so flushed and angry, that the flunkey retires hurriedly in amazement.

Meanwhile poor Cringleby sits down and gets up again, walks about the room, minutely examines the backs of the many books in rows along the walls without knowing one of them, and behaves as nervous men usually do when preparing to take some desperate plunge in life.

Even to take fortune at the flood, requires courage—the water often looks so cold!

No worse or more inopportune moment for asking Sir George a question—great or small—could have been chosen than that selected by the unhappy curate.

To be called a fool by one's own daughter is not calculated to improve the temper, and there is a flush upon the old man's face, and an ominous glitter in his eye, as he enters the library. At the best of times he looks upon the curate as a fool; to-day he is inclined to be enraged with him for coming at all.

"I have called, Sir George," begins poor Cringleby, and then hesitates and finally stops short; reiterating the words, "I have called, Sir George——"

"So I perceive, Mr. Cringleby," says Sir George, with suppressed rage. "He's a bigger fool than I thought him," he thinks.

With a plunge, and more internal postmen busy with whole Valentine's Day deliveries, the curate blunders out: "Called to ask your consent—upon a matter concerning the happiness of two people deeply. I have formed a deep, lasting, and profound attachment for your daughter, Sir George."

At the mention of the word "daughter," the Baronet draws himself up as he stands upon the hearth-rug, and glares with bitter, sarcastic eyes upon the unhappy curate.

"Yes?" he says, with biting satire. "May I inquire which of them has been fortunate enough to win your regard?"

Cringleby, who is standing by an occasional table, grasps it for support as he replies:

"Your younger daughter, Sir George." Poor fellow; he sees all his bright visions fading into nothing before those withering eyes that glance at him so scornfully.

There is a moment's silence, and then Kissingham says quietly:

"I think I grasp your meaning, Mr. Cringleby—this is an application for my daughter Agnes's hand in marriage?"

A ghost of Cringleby's voice murmurs that it is.

"And you think it a fair, honourable, and reasonable proposal, I make no doubt," goes on Sir George, still very softly. "You think that a young lady accustomed all her life to such a home as this" (the Baronet waves his hand over the surrounding magnificence), "such a home as this—would be happy leaving it for your little room over the grocer's shop in the village?"

"I think, sir, that with deep mutual love a hovel becomes a palace."

The elder man laughs a little sarcastic laugh; he rather enjoys the visible trepidation of his visitor.

"Then I can only say, Mr. Cringleby, that your knowledge of the world is exceedingly limited," he says. "I do not ask you what Miss Kissingham's hopes or fears are—I do not care. I have to guard and advance, to the best of my power, the interests of the family—which you are doubtless aware is an old and honoured one. I regret to say that I cannot accept your chimerical theories of sitting-rooms over grocers' shops being palaces. If ever such transformations occur, I congratulate most heartily lodgers *in* grocers' sitting-rooms, but I do not believe it. Therefore, Mr. Cringleby, thanking you for the proposed honour done Miss Kissingham, I beg to refuse your application absolutely, and have pleasure in wishing you good-day."

Sir George rings the bell as he speaks, and before the curate knows where he is, he finds himself walking to his lodgings broken-hearted.

Sir George, extremely upright of carriage, goes

back to his study, feeling that he could write a most cutting article for the magazines on sitting-rooms over grocers' shops becoming palaces by the presence of love, if it were not derogatory to a Kissingham to "do things."

So, instead, he gets out the Kissingham family tree, and sits reading it for a long time; noting how this Kissingham married an earl's daughter, that one a baron's; how this daughter of the house captured a duke, and that a viscount; deriving huge satisfaction from the perusal, and telling himself that, as he often boasted, not one single Kissingham had ever made a *mésalliance*.

Meanwhile, poor Cringleby, with a trembling hand and tearful eye, in his little sitting-room, is penning this sad epistle to his love, to be presently forwarded per the grocer's assistant:

"My dearest Agnes,

"Forget me if you can, though I never shall forget you. Sir George has absolutely refused his consent. Farewell!

"Yours till death,

"Robert Cringleby."

Poor little agitated Agnes, who would as soon think of rebellion as of prussic acid or deadly nightshade, is reading this and weeping, when a tap at her bedroom door makes her start.

"Come in," she says.

Her maid comes in at once, with a startled face, and with another letter in her hand.

"Miss Kissingham went out at half-past five, miss," she says, "in the dark; and when I went upstairs after my tea, I found this note for you," handing it.

It is so unusual for Elinor to go out at half-past five in the winter, and leave notes behind her, that Agnes tears the letter open in wild haste. Casting her eyes over the contents, she gives a little frightened scream, and bursts out crying.

The note is very short and characteristic:

"DEAR OLD AGGIE,

"I'm awfully sorry to startle you, but I can't stand the guv'nor's stupidity any longer. I'm leaving home, and not coming back any more. Tom Slingsby is coming, too. Don't cry or be astonished; he's the jolliest fellow *I've* ever seen. We've got a license and every thing, and are to be married to-morrow morning.

"Yours ever,

"NELL."

It is a long time before Agnes can summon the courage to go to Sir George's study with the letter. When she does so she finds him still busy with the pedigree, and still extremely erect.

"Oh, father!" she cries, "what shall we do?"

Her own trouble is quite obliterated in that she feels for the proud old man.

"I wish particularly, Agnes, to have no scenes," he says, thinking her tears are caused by his refusal of the curate's offer; "I positively refuse my consent. Look here, Agnes, this is our pedigree; please note that not one of the family has ever made a *mésalliance*."

"Oh, father! *one* has *now*," sobs Aggie, handing him Elinor's letter. "Read it. I'm so sorry for you, father."

The old man takes the letter, and reads of his humiliation without a word.

She expected an outbreak of passion, but Sir George is quite silent.

"Will you try to follow them?" she asks at length.

"No. She has taken her course—let her pursue it. You know, I suppose, that I have had Cringleby here to-day?"

A blushing "Yes."

"So you wish to do very little better than your sister—a poor curate and starvation, eh?"

"Oh, father!"

"Answer my question, please—do you wish it?"

Another fluttering, blushing "Yes."

"Very well. That is sufficient. Both my daughters appear equally unsuited to the proud position they hold as Kissinghams. They shall cease to be Kissinghams. I refused Cringleby in your name and my own to-day. I will write at once and say that I consent. No," for the girl makes a caressing gesture; "no. I have done with both my children to-day for ever. Oblige me by leaving the room. I advise you to make all necessary arrangements for your marriage as speedily as possible. I shall not see you again, nor shall I dream of being present at your wedding. Now go."

Sir George points to the door with such an unmistakable look upon his face that the girl, with a last despairing glance of fondness and affection cast behind her, is obliged to go.

Left alone, the old man, taking pen and paper, writes to the lately-rejected one, fierce rage boiling the while beneath his calm exterior:

"Sir,

"I have just learned that my eldest daughter has eloped with, and proposes marrying, her groom. Under these circumstances, should you still, knowing all, wish to contract a marriage with my second daughter, I withdraw the refusal I gave this afternoon, though I absolutely decline to see either her or you again. Miss Agnes Kissingham knows my determination.

"Yours, etc.,

"George Kissingham."

When Sir George has written and despatched this letter, he proceeds to lock up the pedigree with a sigh; he will not refer to it again at present.

What a whirl of varied emotions come to the dumbfoundment of poor Cringleby with the receipt of Sir George's letter!

Then in a wild ecstasy of love the grocery assistant

is brought into requisition again as bearer of the following despatch:

"MY DEAREST AGNES,

"Never forget me, and burn my last letter. Sir George has given his consent absolutely. I don't know what it all means—only that I am the happiest man breathing. Tell me, by return of the assistant in the shop who brings this, when and where I may see you. Oh, do let it be soon, dearest.
"Yours till death,
"ROBERT CRINGLEBY."

Some things happen fortuitously in this wicked world, that is so often, alas, but one of cross-purposes, and it turns out that Robert has a dear old capped and curled maiden aunt living mildly near Paddington Station. She receives Agnes with open arms. Cringleby obtains a substitute for the Rome-and-water services at Kissingham for the remainder of his engagement, and hies him to London gaily. Within the shortest time compatible with legality, there are a blushing little bride and a happy bridegroom one day at a certain church in the Marylebone Road; and the dear old smiling maiden aunt gives herself a headache upon cheap sherry, drinking eternal happiness to the loving couple.

"When we come back from Southsea, I shall certainly call upon Lord Maidenhair," says the bridegroom, when the lowly growler is at the door that afternoon, and forthwith drives off straight into Paradise with Agnes.

CHAPTER VIII.

"THE WOOING O'T."

SIR GEORGE KISSINGHAM, Baronet, having by his own act disposed of his only remaining daughter, and, as he thinks, by his manner of doing it delivered a nasty stab to her husband, begins to feel entirely satisfied with himself. In view of that step he is not yet absolutely committed to, but which he has made up his mind now to take, daughters, or even one daughter, he reflects, would be extremely inconvenient in many ways. At its first impact the blow was a heavy one to him. In his heart he nourished ambitious hopes of seeing his elder girl a peeress, and his younger daughter's son perhaps adopting the Kissingham name and arms in a dim, wealthy future.

It matters little who you are—duke or dustman—when you have cherished a hope a long time, the annihilation of it is deeply painful. But fortunately for Sir George's happiness, there is a dash of selfishness in the Kissingham blood. Though his hopes are destroyed utterly, there still remains the fact that some ten or fifteen years of his own life have to be clothed in not only undiminished, but if anything increasing, luxury.

Had he been a richer man, Sir George at this juncture would undoubtedly have wooed a youthful beauty, and achieved the perpetuation of his name. Under existing circumstances this he knows to be hopeless. He must marry money, and the only money likely to marry him is, alas! elderly money. He knows his fate perfectly. He wishes, perhaps, it had less false youth and more of honest age about it, but it cannot be helped. 'Tis destiny.

My Lady Netherby, scientifically tuned to concert pitch, is in her youthful boudoir this afternoon, trying to feel bashful, and fluttered, and foolish (succeeding only in the latter), cause being a letter from Sir George, stating the writer's intention of calling at four o'clock, and begging for a private interview, which has been accorded by return of post.

"If Sir George Kissingham calls, show him in, and I shall be at home to no one else to-day," the Netherby has told her gorgeous flunkey, who has straightway joined his fellows below stairs with the intelligence that there's "a something hup between them two old fools, for a guinea."

It is not always the lot of captivating woman to know the exact hour at which the thief cometh who shall endeavour to appropriate her heart. If she *does* know, as the cavalry man examines girths and bridle, and loosens his sword in its scabbard whilst waiting for the word "Charge," so in exactly similar spirit does the woman expecting a proposal—be she sixteen or sixty—cast a glance over her traps and accoutrements before the fray. Lady Netherby has everything arranged in her girlish little boudoir for conquest. She is sitting on the sofa, and not on her usual chair—sitting on her sofa with a suggestively reserved place for one between herself and the fire. Such a cosy, cushioned, artful seat, well-nigh compelling occupancy by any one looking at it. All around are those thousand unnameable trifles, which contribute so much more than we are wont to imagine to the spell feminine. In my lady's hands some fancy work, often laid down to be replaced by a fire-screen, each movement of which wafts abroad spicy breezes, sweeter than any blowing soft o'er Ceylon's isle. Upon my lady's cheek that artistic blush we have seen there before, deepened somewhat in anticipation of what it *should* be. At my lady's feet are skins, softer than swan's-down; on a distant table a shaded lamp, supported by an alabaster Venus, blushing at her task.

In such manner does my lady dispose her available forces on this memorable day.

Very frequently does my lady glance towards the cunning little clock nestling casually amongst the ornaments upon the mantelpiece; glance towards it and speculate how far *wrong* it may be, for this delicate piece of workmanship partakes somewhat of the nature of its mistress in the matter of not always telling the exact advance of time.

The yards-long footman brings cessation to this speculation presently with the announcement of the expected visitor.

Sir George has on his best-fitting frock-coat, and evinces a careful regard for his first-Duke-of-Wellington appearance; otherwise he has about him something of the air of a conscious victor taking a "walk over" the matrimonial course. Still, he is a bit nervous.

"It is very cold to-day, Lady Netherby," is his opening remark.

"Oh yes! quite too dreadfully cold—come nearer the fire," with an enticing gesture to the corner seat of the sofa.

"I thank you, I prefer to stand," replies the Baronet, who feels courage prefers an upright position.

The suitor looks gloomy in spite of his surroundings. Probably he feels what we have mentioned before as coming to most visitors to that girlish boudoir—the wish that the owner of it were more what she pretends to be; the horrible incongruity of it all.

There is an awkward pause. Her ladyship is no utter fool. Something tells her that she had best not be too gushing and youthful with this nibbling fish.

Silence broken by Sir George:

"I have no idea, Lady Netherby, whether you know the object of my visit to-day." (Slight pause, but my lady is looking coyly in the fire.) "I have no idea whether when you honoured me by visiting the Manor you gathered something of the state of—of my feelings?"

He was going to say "heart," but somehow the word stuck in his throat, and refused to come forth.

"Oh, Sir George!" (in a flutter).

"In fact, I have come here to-day to speak plainly

—to place my name at your disposal, my happiness at your feet. The name—the old name of Kissingham is not one to be ashamed of—the family is essentially an honourable one."

"Oh, Sir George!" (doubtingly).

"I trust you will not prolong my suspense unnecessarily. Attachments are—difficult to speak about—but I trust my future in your hands. I ask you to be my wife; will you make my happiness assured by saying yes?"

"From the first day I saw you I have—respected you—and now—now——" says her youthful ladyship, dwindling off into a bashful sigh.

"And now"—advancing and taking her hand—"and now you will accept, dear Lady Netherby?"

What a coy little stammering "yes" that is! But it answers the purpose. Sir George advances and presses her hand to his lips, saying:

"Elizabeth—your name *is* Elizabeth, I think?"

"But I am always *called* Lizzie."

"I seldom adopt abbreviations—there is a degree of familiarity about them which I dislike—you will not object, I hope, to be called Elizabeth?"

"It's fearfully *dowdy*, isn't it?—George—oh! how strange it seems to call you George! and really quite improper—but I suppose it's not, is it? You must tell me if you think it is, won't you?"

Sir George agrees to do this willingly, and heaves a deep, deep sigh, half relief, half sadness. He has won the day, but the cost is great.

In an awkward, mechanical way he sits down beside his future wife. "I hope—I trust we shall be happy. I believe we shall," he says. "You are doubtless aware that both my daughters have left my protection?"

"Yes, I *have* heard. I am so greatly sorry for you, poor George." She lays her hand upon his sleeve caressingly.

"As we are upon this subject, Elizabeth, I will say at once that it must never again be mentioned by you, and it will assuredly never be referred to by me. They have proved themselves unworthy of the name they bore. They bear it no longer. They are dead to me."

"Oh, George!"

"It is very painful to me to have to speak thus—extremely painful; but I feel speaking explicitly and at once will save much unpleasantness in the future. You understand?"

Of course she does, and says so.

The old man sighs again. It is rather a dreary wooing, on the whole.

He feels it a relief when he can go to his club to dinner.

As for youthful Liz, she dashes off a tiny note, in the highest of high spirits, to her dear Bessie, and tells her that "all is settled, they will be married very soon, and that Sir George is a *love*—absolutely a *love*, my dear!"

"Here's a game, Henry!" exclaims Mrs. Bingham, bursting into her husband's study and disturbing his cogitations of formations. "Here's a game, Henry! The old boy has been fool enough to propose, and they're positively going to be married! Isn't it an excellent joke?"

Matching unfortunate couples is an exciting and enthralling game to Mrs. Bingham, and she always plays it utterly regardless of consequences.

But, when the note that calls forth this keen delight in Mrs. Bingham's heart has been despatched, my Lady Netherby rings her bell and requests that Chipps may be sent to her. Chipps, who is as old as her mistress, has a hard, fierce face with a pair of piercing, fiery eyes, that have somehow an unpleasant, devouring expression in them. Years of service have brought about a certain familiarity between the two—a familiarity which, to judge from Chipps's face as she comes into the room now, has bred contempt. Strangely enough, too, my lady looks at her with a sort of fear, and simpers:

"Chipps, don't look so angry; I've something to tell you."

"I can guess it," replies Chipps, stolidly. "You're going to befool *this* man now."

"Oh, really, Chipps! You naughty, unpleasant thing, you. What do you mean?"

Chipps answers the question by a glance only, but before it my lady's eyes fall at once. "Oh, really, Chipps—really, you know," she says, deprecatingly, "you're horrible, and you can leave the room—there!"

"I will leave it, though I will never leave *you*," answers the maid, with sudden anger and a flash of her piercing eyes. "Never!"

"How devoted you are!" my lady replies, with an attempt—but a very poor one—at gaiety. But Chipps has gone out.

CHAPTER IX.

TAKES THE UNHEARD-OF LIBERTY OF ACCOMPANYING A HAPPY PAIR UPON THEIR HONEYMOON.

ELINOR KISSINGHAM did not speak at random when she told her sister that she and her lover had a "license and everything" ready for the flight they proposed taking. Everything *was* ready, and the marriage took place in London the morning after leaving the Manor.

"Now I don't care a halfpenny for any one, Tom. Where shall we lunch?" said that practical young lady, as they came out of church after the ceremony, man and wife.

Tom, who is not half such a bad sort of fellow, and feels terribly happy at his good fortune, suggests that perhaps the "Criterion" would be as convenient a place as any other for purposes of refreshment.

Thither, therefore, this strange couple repair forthwith, and over the luncheon and some claret decide upon their next step.

"I'm only sorry at leaving the horses, though we couldn't afford to keep them, that's certain," says Mrs. Slingsby, busy, with an appetite in no way disconcerted by excitement, upon a cutlet. "We shall have a pretty close fit of it on our two hundred a year; but I've a hundred or two in hand, and we'll have a bit of an outing somewhere; the thing we've got to decide now is where to go."

"It doesn't matter a bit to me," answers her husband. "I suppose the seaside is *the* thing."

"Well, name the place; we'll start for it in half an hour. Is there any special place you'd like to see?"

Tom's earliest days, it seems, were spent at Brighton. He would like immensely to revisit the place he hasn't seen since his childhood.

"That's easily managed; we'll go to Brighton this afternoon," answers Elinor, readily.

So *that* is settled.

"We shan't be able to afford hotels, it's a case of lodgings," Mrs. Slingsby decides as they are speeding southward. "And they are more comfortable, too. I hate hotels!"

So *that* is settled.

There is very generally considerable difficulty about selecting lodgings. Either the rooms are dark, or the landlady forbidding, or the servant dirty, to say nothing of the prices asked being absurdly high. Every one knows all these inconveniences; amongst others, Mrs. Slingsby, who tells the flyman whom she hails at the station to drive to the eastern portion of the town.

"I'm going Kemp Town way for two reasons, Tom," she tells her husband as they proceed in that direction. "Firstly, because it is cheap, and secondly, because, as you say your early days were passed in that locality, I think you'll prefer it."

Tom states, in language of devotion, that though any place with his wife's company would be happy to him, still, from boyish recollections, Kemp Town will be especially so.

By direction of Mrs. Slingsby, the fly stops at a small post-office, which is also a baker's shop, boasting groves of bread spotless as virgin modesty.

"Always go to a post-office for information as to lodgings," says Elinor, getting out of the fly. One would imagine she had engaged apartments by the score ere this, to see her matter-of-fact behaviour.

In response to a tap of Mrs. Slingsby's foot upon the floor, a bright, sharp-eyed little woman of forty, dressed in black, with a white apron, darts out of the parlour behind the shop with surprising briskness, and inquires:

"Is it stamps, ma'am?"

"No, it's lodgings," answers Elinor, smiling.

"Oh! yes. So many people want stamps, that's why I asked you," says the little sharp-eyed woman, leaning her elbows upon the counter in a confidential manner, and continuing: "But it's lodgings; how many rooms, ma'am?"

Mrs. Slingsby mentions her modest requirements.

"Now, let me see," says the little sharp-eyed woman, reflectively, staring very hard at the scales and weights upon the counter for inspiration. Before they have afforded her this, her reverie is interrupted by a small girl, hungry for a 'arf-quartern, "and stale, mother says, if you please, marm."

That handing the loaf to the small customer apparently gives the inspiration required by the occasion, for the little woman says suddenly, as the child disappears:

"The very thing; but perhaps you would object to Dissent, ma'am?"

"I don't quite catch your meaning, Mrs. Cripps," says Elinor, who has read the name on some paper bags of assorted sizes hanging behind the sharp-eyed little woman.

"Why, marm, I know of just the rooms to suit you, clean and airy and *with* a bow-window, close by, but they belong to the minister of the Methodist Chapel round the corner, Mr. Tipgrace. But then, he won't get a-preaching to you, marm," finishes Mrs. Cripps, "and the bow-window is excellent."

The bow-window seems to cover a multitude of sins in Mrs. Cripps' sharp little eyes.

Elinor says at once that the keeper of the lodgings may be a Jew, Turk, or infidel, for all she cares, so long as the rooms are clean and airy, and starts off with her husband to explore Mr. Tipgrace's apartments.

They are close by, and easily found. Mr. Tipgrace is a bachelor presiding over and assisting the upward tendencies of the souls appertaining to the bodies of some hundred and fifty persons "sitting under him," as he puts it. The arrangements do not take long to make. Mr. Tipgrace charges only a little more than his rooms are honestly worth, and then, too, "the bow-window has to be considered," as Elinor says.

"What does it matter where we are, so long as we're together, and the roof's watertight?" Tom asks feelingly; and we have it in our heart to reply from the bottom of it, "nothing." What does *anything* matter in this dreary old world so long as our darling is with us, even leaving the roof out of the question altogether?

"I don't think he's such a terribly bad sort after all," says Elinor, laughing. "He anoints his hair, and wears it a bit long, but comparing him with old Saintly, who wears his *coat* long, instead of his hair, I don't see much to choose between them. Of course, neither of them is to be compared with Cringleby, who *won't* wear his coat *or* his hair long, and who is something of a man. It's your nondescripts I hate! I don't mind a Roman Catholic priest, and I don't mind a Protestant clergyman; but I can *not* stand a cross between the two."

Elinor has it all her own way, evidently. But Tom is utterly and completely happy, and that is a great deal. They both have that most glorious of all attributes—youth. They are a long time busy arranging their rooms, and afterwards there is an excursion to be made into the town for necessaries, and it is all so novel and delightful. The future, seen in the golden light of morning, cannot fail to look bright. Suppose they *have* to endure poverty, why, they are together, and the roof is watertight.

CHAPTER X.

MRS. SAINTLY TRIMS A LITTLE.

IT is not for a moment to be supposed that the events we have described in the latter chapters produced no excitement in and about Kissingham and elsewhere. There was immense excitement and gossip, of course.

Baronets' daughters do not elope with their grooms every day in the week, though such flights have ere this been known. Neither do Baronets' younger daughters suddenly wed impecunious curates up in London within a few days of their engagement being public property. The Kissingham household gossiped, Kissingham village gossiped; but to a certain extent, the two events—and especially when followed by the announcement of Sir George's proposed marriage—nullified each other. It is very difficult even for villages to be wildly excited about two or three things at one and the same time. At length, the whole matter resolved itself into speculation as to what sort of lady the Netherby, when a Kissingham, would be in the neighbourhood.

We have said that a deep dislike to her ladyship

sprang up in the heart of Mrs. Saintly, when the former refused to subscribe to some local charity. When once a woman has taken a deep dislike to any one, no mitigating circumstance can be adduced to cause her to alter her opinion. There is no such hate in the world as a woman's hate. This is why, at the Vicarage tea-table this afternoon, Mrs. Saintly is saying to her quiet, inoffensive husband:

"Whatever Sir George can be about to think of such a marriage, I can't imagine! It's perfectly amazing—a horrible, stingy, got-up thing like her!"

"Really, my dear—a cup more tea, please—perhaps Sir George likes her."

"Then he's more of a fool than I took him for, if he does," snaps the Vicaress, bitterly. "Mark my words, there's something very strange about that woman."

"In the head, my dear?"

"In the head? No! In the character. She's right enough in the *head*, a great deal too right there. I hate a woman who is too sharp, and Lady Netherby certainly is. She refused to give me only a sovereign for my mothers' meetings."

"Probably she will, now that this parish is become *her* parish, my dear."

"I hope she will, for her own sake; it will be remarkably unpleasant for her if she doesn't," says Mrs. Saintly, with a tone that adds, "if I can make it so."

"We should be charitable, Maria."

"That's just the thing I'm finding fault with her for, if you had any perceptive faculties, Mr. Saintly," says his wife, with great bitterness—"*she won't* be charitable, I regret to say. She refused—positively refused—to subscribe to my mothers' meetings—the meetings that have done so much good in the place, and at which I learn so much of what is going on around us—learn where I can be of assistance, I mean."

"Some people I know object to mothers' meetings on principle—thinking there is gossip talked at them," ventures Mr. Saintly, meekly. In the depths of his heart he has some such suspicion himself.

"How can I help *that*?" demands his wife, with great severity. "Don't some misguided, ignorant people object to your ornamental services?"

"I must confess, my dear——" begins Saintly, in an extremely low voice, when his wife interrupts him with vehemence:

"I will *not* have you get in this way of arguing about everything; it's a habit that grows on one very fast. You now argue everything I say. I tell you simply, that this Lady Netherby is a most objectionable woman, with—I have reason to believe—a doubtful past."

"Her husband, the late Lord Netherby, was Hereditary Grand *Bon-bon* Puller of England, my dear."

"So he may have been; but I don't see why that should vouch for the character of the woman he married. Debrett says she was daughter of —— Tebbs, Esq. Does *that* sound respectable? Daughter of a man with a Christian name evidently of such an objectionable nature that Debrett refuses to mention it."

Mr. Saintly always has been afraid of his wife; he, therefore, only says feebly now:

"It does *not* look very satisfactory, certainly, my dear."

"I wonder you admit as much as that, with your awkward habit of contradicting me at every turn," says the lady; "and how many more cups of tea are you thinking of drinking? This is your third!"

"I should like *one* more, making four, if you don't mind," replies the Vicar, meekly. "It is very cold to-night—the weather, I mean," he adds quickly, lest he should draw down domestic wrath by accusing the tea.

Mrs. Saintly is in the act of handing the fourth cup, with a very bad grace, when a very resounding ring comes at the front-door bell.

"I fancy that must be Sir George," says the Vicar, drinking off his tea hurriedly.

This surmise proves correct. Sir George is ushered into the room almost immediately.

"Oh, Sir George!" exclaims Mrs. Saintly, when she and her husband have shaken the visitor's hand warmly. "Oh, Sir George! I haven't seen you since the last pleasant news in the *Post*. So you really *are* going to venture into matrimonial harness again—and such a charming partner, too. I thought her the most interesting person I have ever seen—in a sense. I wish you every happiness!" And the dear lady shakes hands again in sheer good-nature.

"I thank you sincerely for your kindness and good wishes. I am glad you like Lady Netherby. I hope she may prove—I am sure she will prove—an acquisition to the neighbourhood," says the Baronet, in his cold, even tones. Turning a little, he catches a look of dire confusion on the Vicar's face, which he cannot quite understand — he has not heard Mrs. Saintly's previous conversation as we have.

"Depend upon it, there is nothing like matrimony for a man," goes on this worthy lady, quite overflowing with benevolence. "It makes a man *a* man. I feel deeply for *all* unmarried men."

Catching sight of the Vicar again just at this point, Sir George fancies he sees something in the priestly face more than the usual meekness; something which seems to say that Mr. Saintly does not quite agree with his wife's theory on this subject.

"I should describe marriage as a great privilege," the happy husband says, feeling that Sir George expects something of him. "A great privilege. Not to be lightly taken in hand or abandoned."

"Exactly. Indeed, it is rather a difficult thing *to* abandon," says the visitor, drily. He is thinking that more people would be willing to take it in hand, perhaps, if there *were* the possibility *of* abandoning it if necessary.

Presently Sir George and the Vicar adjourn to the latter's study, as there is some magisterial business to be discussed. Before getting to work, however, the Baronet is once more heartily congratulated by Mrs. Saintly upon his coming happiness. She is sure, she says, Lady Kissingham and herself will be *great* friends.

That perplexed look comes upon the Vicar's face again.

When the Baronet has driven off in his brougham, to which he has been attended by the Vicar in all humility, the latter comes into the little room, from which tea has now been cleared away, and looks at his wife—still with perplexity written on his face.

"I think, my dear—I really *do* think——" he says in a deprecating tone.

"What *do* you think?" asks his wife, with the suppressed anger of one who feels guilty.

"I think, my dear, you—were just a trifle, my dear —only a trifle, you know—insincere."

"Insincere! hark at him!" cries the lady, appealing to vacancy. "Insincere because I made myself agreeable to Sir George! What nonsense will you talk next?"

"You said, my dear, that you were sure Lady Kissingham and yourself would be great friends."

"And so we shall be, if she is more liberal. I'm the great friend of *all* liberal people. You wouldn't have had me do the woman the injustice of imagining that she *won't* be liberal, would you?" demands the lady, with great bitterness.

"I know that we clergy, sometimes, have to—to trim our sails considerably—the Church always *has* trimmed her sails; but still, my dear, I don't wish to annoy you, but you certainly *did* trim very considerably indeed."

"It was for the cause," says Mrs. Saintly, with resignation. "I am obliged to outrage my feelings sometimes for the cause. I would not quarrel with any lady whom Sir George might bring to the Manor. I think of all my poor suffering mothers. What could I do but trim—for the cause, you know?"

"Oh! *for the cause*," says the Vicar, mollified considerably. "Yes, it *was* for the cause, and for that, of course, we must do anything. Perhaps, my love, as it *was* for the cause, you did perfectly right—I'm sure I hope so." And Mr. Saintly drops off into a quiet doze by the fire, and dreams — whatever parsons do dream of—bishoprics, perhaps.

Half an hour later he fancies—but he must be dreaming still—he hears his wife saying: "All the same, she *is* a detestable woman, and I pity poor Sir George from the bottom of my heart."

CHAPTER XI.

"THE WEDDING O'T."

WITH a spring sunshine stealing in at the tracery windows of a certain West End church, and gathering colour from the rainbow saints upon the glass, to fleck the tablets and the tombs with varied hues.

With a great crowd of fashionables assembled, partly from friendship, partly from amused curiosity.

With five reporters from Society papers, hungry for detail, in a gallery.

With a wondering crowd outside who point out Sir George to each other as the "father o' the bride."

With a white satin gown of virgin purity, and with, oh! such a fluttered, girlish little smile upon her lips, does my Lady Netherby come to plight her troth to Kissingham of Kissingham.

Mr. and Mrs. Bingham, the latter especially, seem very much in the foreground of the picturesque group at the fatal rails; she is taking everything in, and enjoying it all thoroughly. As for Mr. Bingham, he is unfortunately placed so that a great blotch of colour from the stained window falls upon his bald head, looking like some hideous bruise.

There is, too, a sickly shade of yellow for an instant on my lady's face, but she shifts her place a trifle, and the great orange streak falls slantingly upon the matting of the aisle, with no worse result than giving the appearance of tawny socks to a gentleman in Oxford shoes.

The great rolling notes of the organ die away, and the sing-song voice of Mr. Saintly (brought up, carriage paid, for the occasion) becomes audible in the opening sentences of the service.

My Lord Maidenhair is present, standing near Daisy Saintly, his attraction somewhat diverted from the service by a large dusty cobweb visible in an angle of the roof.

A smart young gentleman standing close beside a smart young lady, whispers her behind his prayer-book, "Wonderful symmetry of bone!" alluding to the hand my lady puts forth, ungloved, at the moment to receive the golden badge of marriage; and the smart young lady, with a glance, murmurs to the flowers in her breast, "How I pity *both!*" A remark which the smart young gentleman apparently thinks uncommonly funny, for he smiles a reply.

Old Admiral Corfew (college chum of the bridegroom's), standing quite at the back of the group, and leaning his stout frame against the side of a pew, is holding quite a suppressed conversation with General Marches (retired), upon the subject of marriage late in life, and saying, below his breath:

"It's a mistake, Bill, depend upon it—a mistake after forty, if it isn't an indiscretion before. Look at me; I've never married. See the flesh I carry—no bothers, my boy, no henpeckings; that's it. Though the service is gone to—never mind where, in this place—I'll tell you when we get outside—I've not lost flesh."

And General Marches, in a husky voice, replies: "Hang me if I don't think you're right, Bob. I've been married three times, and I believe they got worse each time. If it weren't for my girl there—the sole survivor, as I may say, barring myself—I should be exactly of your opinion; but she *is* a strapping fine gal, ain't she?" And the old man looks proudly at the identical young lady who was whispering to her bouquet just now.

"A smart craft, I'll admit," says the Admiral, looking in the indicated direction. "But lor, Bill, you should see the gals we used to be mad about in the Bermudas! Such eyes, sir! Sitting with them of a dark night you'd catch yourself just about to light your cigar from 'em, they shone so bright, I give you my word. And then, *such* figures!—Look out, the job's over!"

It is, and the organ pealing the Wedding March—"to drown the cries of the victims," the smart young lady says.

There is a partial trooping into the vestry, and a partial grouping of gossips in the church.

Register signed in due form, and witnessed.

Such a driving up and off of carriages to Mrs. Bingham's, where the breakfast is spread!

Such a prancing of horses and banging of doors!

Such laughing faces! To see it all, you would imagine sweet seventeen had just wedded lusty five-and-twenty, instead of the dreary fact. Even at the top sparkle of her glory to-day my lady looks a little ghastly: what she really is when her maid has taken her to pieces, like a puzzle, at night, it is impossible to imagine.

"No, but really, doesn't she make up *cleverly?*" asks the before-mentioned smart young lady of her male companion during breakfast. "Look at her; it's most artistic."

"Netherby married her off the boards," replies the man; "that's why she's so good at 'getting up,' I imagine."

So in undertones the fair Lizzie is dissected and criticised by most of the guests, as she innocently sits behind a silvered cake of gigantic proportions, bedizened with emblematic love all over. Presently there is a silence upon the company, for Mr. Bingham is proposing the health of the bride and bridegroom.

It is needless to give his speech. His only public utterances occur before the Committee of the Royal Geological Society, and he cannot exactly keep in view that he is otherwise employed now; the consequence being that he makes surprising allusions to "Mr. Chairman," and apologises immediately.

Mrs. Bingham appears to look upon the whole affair as a sort of private theatricals, provided for her own especial amusement, and is in the best spirits imaginable.

Sir George responds to the toast his host proposes

in a staid, elderly, mechanical speech, suggesting more than ever the mechanical Baronet (Debrett's Patent). There is rippling small-talk during my lady's change of costume for the journey to Paris; audible agreement between the Admiral and the General that England and the world together are going very rapidly to the dogs. Then carriages come up, and Lady Kissingham comes down, there is the banging of a carriage-door, and the disappearance of Sir George and his wife into the oblivion of matrimonial bliss amid a shower of rice.

"It's the best thing of the sort I've ever done," laughs Mrs. Bingham to her husband, when the whole thing is over, and the guests gone. "Unhesitatingly the *very* best! And I'll tell you what, Henry, we'll go to the theatre together to-night—yes, we will—though I'm sure we shan't see anything funnier than what I've shown you to-day." With which truthful remark dear Bessie allows her husband to attend to his "formations" till dinner-time.

CHAPTER XII.

MILVERDALE VICARAGE.

THE great loom of Fate has woven its mysterious pattern for six months or more. The Reaper has been busy amongst the human corn-fields, and amongst other grain fallen before his sickle is the Vicar of Milverdale, a little parish all rural simplicity, lying in a leafy nest amid the hills down Muddlebury way.

Lord Maidenhair, in whose gift, we have said before, the living is, does not forget that promise made to Robert Cringleby over the beetle-case. Within a year of his marriage with Aggie, the Reverend Robert finds himself installed in his vicarial office, and wildly happy.

Milverdale Vicarage is the brightest, cosiest, most cheery Vicarage—or, for that matter, abode of any sort—in all the Midlands. On a tiny scale, certainly, but none the worse for that circumstance. It is the size of the heart, and not of the house, thank God, that constitutes happiness, after all.

The Vicarage is a little, low, thatched abode, separated only by a low wall from the churchyard, but facing, away over undulating meadows, to the horizon. There is a little garden, which Agnes loves to plant with the old English flowers which are so fast passing away from us to oblivion. There is a little rambling stable, wherein abides the fat pony that draws the little chaise in which Robert and his wife make their parochial calls and do their Saturday's marketing in Muddlebury, as blithe and loving a couple as any in England.

Not a villager but sees the Vicar's face, with a cheery greeting on it, at least once a week, not counting the Sunday service.

Truly, there are no great people near at hand, and that a dinner with Farmer Welsh, parson's warden, constitutes the chief gaiety of the place. But then, as Agnes often says, they only want each other's society, and that is always attainable.

To-night the curtains are close drawn in the snug little parlour, the fire blazing, and a dog and cat, the greatest friends in the world, sleeping side by side upon the hearth-rug.

Tea-things are upon a side-table, and a plate of steaming muffins placed within the fender to keep warm. That dear little matronly woman sitting beside the fire, with some sewing in her hand, is Agnes. The plump little hands work wonders of rapid manipulation with her work, though frequently she stops to listen, for Robert is out upon his visiting rounds, and the wind has risen somewhat fiercely, making the fire roar and crackle ever and anon as the gale flutters at the chimney-top like some huge bird.

Now Agnes rises, and turns up the lamp a trifle, and before she sits down places the Vicar's slippers within the ruddy glow of the fire to warm. What a happy face she has! What a thrice happy man is Robert Cringleby to own such a wife!

Presently there is the sound of wheels outside, and Agnes starts up and flies to open the hall-door. The next moment she is coming in again, with her hand upon her Robert's arm, and a colour a trifle heightened—it looks as though, in the dim light of the tiny hall, he has kissed her.

The Vicar has abandoned all his "High" pomps and vanities, and is arrayed in black velveteens, well fitting.

Altogether Robert Cringleby looks stouter, and more manly, and more happy than when at Kissingham.

No wonder! The acquiring of such a wife as Agnes should improve any man's appearance.

"How is Nancy?" is the little matron's first question, when the warmed slippers are on, and the tea-table drawn up between them before the fire.

"Well — really better. I think now she will recover," answers the Vicar, taking the cup the dainty little hand holds out to him in a way which says, "Detain me too for a moment, if you like." He takes the hint, and the blush comes to the happy wife's hand as she withdraws it from his fond, loving pressure.

"I'm so glad she's better. I began to fear. And fancy, Robert, you've not had one funeral since we've been here!"

"Well, darling, that is only four months, and our population under six hundred."

"The books from the Muddlebury Library have come—the butcher brought them. It's very good of him. They will all do anything for us," says Agnes, smiling.

"I don't wonder at any one doing anything for *you*, dearest," replies the Vicar, with a glance of affection. "All the books we ordered?"

"Yes, the whole of them. So you can begin reading to me to-night."

"But I thought we had agreed that *you* were to do the reading, Aggie?"

"Yes—we did, I know," with a hesitation and a blush, "we did, I know—but, in fact, Robert—it is imperative that this work should be finished," says Agnes, speaking the words very fast, and with a deeper blush.

"Then, darling, I'll read, of course," answers the young husband, glancing at her with a smile; but she is bending down very low to feed the dog, and so he cannot see her face.

He rises presently, and reaching down a pipe and tobacco-jar, begins to fill the former. Agnes loves smoke, she avers, and Robert has acquired this habit along with his new-born happiness.

A neat little village maid comes in in response to the ringing of a bell, and clears away the tea equipage. When all is done and the servant gone, the Vicar goes to a table and looks over the new library books. Selecting one at length, he brings it back with him to his chair beside the fire, and places it, open at the first page, upon his knee.

"But I can't read and smoke too," he says, laughing.

"Then let's talk instead," says his wife, looking up from the important work in her lap. "Let us talk over old times and the old village."

So they fall to beating that ground which never to true lovers becomes barren, of how, when, and where they first became acquainted, and what each thought of the other then.

Such a talk is none the less dear because pauses occur in it frequently, each going deep down into those secret places in the heart which no loving intimacy can ever quite find words to talk about. So sacred are they that instinctively the voice dies away to silence as beside the new-made grave of those we love.

"I am only sorry for one thing, Robert," says Agnes at length, breaking one of such silences.

"And that is?"

"That father will not forgive us."

"Time, dearest, may do even that. I am sure Maidenhair has done all in his power to bring about a reconciliation."

"I'm so sorry for father—about Nell. That must have been a terrible blow to him. You have no conception how proud he is. The thought of a Kissingham marrying a groom was agony to him, I'm certain," and Agnes sighs.

"His marriage may occupy his thoughts now," suggests the Vicar.

"Oh, how I trust it may!" exclaims the daughter, earnestly.

Then there is another long silence, broken only by the roaring of the wind without, and the snoring of the dog within.

"If time and Lord Maidenhair *can't* effect a forgiveness of us—what then?" asks the wife, presently.

"I think I know what will do it even then."

"Oh, Robert, do you really—what?"

"When I write to him."

"But you have already written, and he has not replied."

"I mean, dearest, when I write, as I shall do soon, and tell him that——"

"Oh, what?" is all Agnes answers, but she jumps up, and flinging her arms about his neck, sobs tears that are April ones only, half joy, half sorrow.

"Surely a child to live and bear the name—for it shall be christened Kissingham—will win his heart, darling."

"I hardly dare to hope even that, he is so proud and cold," sobs Agnes, still with her arms about her husband's neck.

"Wait and see, darling — wait and see, and — really, my pipe is out again—it must be your tears, Agnes." And the happy Vicar strikes a match vigorously to rekindle his tobacco, smoking on again when it is alight with a fond eye resting on his wife.

It seems no time at all before the little village maiden is in the room again, spreading a snowy cloth for supper, and drawing the table within the cheery circle of the fire's ruddy glow. For pleasure always trips with flying feet which leave no impress behind, even as sorrow stamps each lagging footfall on our weary heart!

"My only sorrow is that we cannot go on like this for ever and ever," says the Vicar, enthusiastically, before they sit down.

Agnes has moved away to the window and drawn aside the curtain, looking out upon a drifted, frightened moon speeding through banks of cloud. Her only answer, made with one hand upon her husband's shoulder, is to point silently upward.

"True, darling, I was wrong," says the Vicar, leading her to the table. "I was wrong; but my prayer is that each erring mortal, too happy here, may have as fair a guide beside him to the end, pointing skyward."

CHAPTER XIII.

SKELETONS.

ALL these months of married life have not brought a happier expression to Sir George's face, as he sits at luncheon with his wife this Sunday afternoon in the Manor morning-room.

The first-Duke-of-Wellington appearance is still carefully studied and preserved, but there is a lining and furrowing of the face deeper than in days gone by.

My lady, with her dress a trifle more in keeping with her age than when we saw her last, but still fearfully youthful, has the artistic blush delicately painted on her cheeks, and the false eyebrows carefully defined.

They don't know each other, husband and wife, more intimately than when first they met. Their life is still a protracted, weary lie.

Sir George hides from his partner how terribly the upholding of the Kissingham magnificence has reduced the Kissingham property. My lady conceals from her husband all those little artifices and instruments with which she vainly tries to clog the wheels of time.

My lady in her suite of apartments, Sir George in *his*, have very little in common beside their name. Guests come and go at the Manor; visits are paid, and dinners given in return; all heartless, cynic hospitality, dreary in the extreme to witness. County magnates go away in their broughams after the Manor entertainments, shivering beneath their luxurious fur rugs—shivering, but more with horror than with cold.

There are a sacerdotal butler and a plush flunkey attending the luncheon-table to-day, though there are no visitors. But there are no secrets to be talked between husband and wife, apparently.

Sir George, deep in thought, eats his cutlet mechanically; my lady plays with a wing of chicken, and thinks longingly of the liquid tuning apparatus she will use so freely later.

The silence is oppressive for some time; even the extent of making audible the somewhat thick breathing of the portly butler. Then my lady, feeling that something must be done for the sake of appearances, simpers dentistically:

"A large congregation at church to-day, George? I was afraid of the cold wind, or *I* should have gone. I positively have not been to church for two Sundays."

Sir George, with a face which says how terribly weary he is of all this ghastliness, answers shortly:

"A small congregation; Saintly preached," as

though this latter fact had some bearing upon the former one.

"I'm not surprised. I like the curate best," replies youthful Lizzie.

Another long silence; with the lady vaguely wondering how long ago it is since anybody liked *her*—really and truly liked her; thinking she would give all she possesses to be able to rekindle the old light in men's eyes, the old softness of their voices.

Sir George is abstracted, too, but from a different cause. There is a spectre close beside him always now, sleeping and waking: RUIN!

He has been struggling with his pride for months past to make a request to his wife for money—a great deal of money—to put things straight that have become horribly crooked.

At the present moment his energies are directed to the staving off of the evil day, and he has partially succeeded in this. If he can keep the mortgagees and his other creditors in good humour with occasional sops, he may be able to run his dreary course another year yet. But the strain upon him is terrible. The bare thought of a Kissingham in such a strait is well-nigh unendurable to his nature.

Rashleigh, the family solicitor, importuned constantly by his client as to a way out of his difficulties, has repeated over and over again of late the same advice: "Apply to my lady."

"That is my very last resource," Sir George has replied always. "When there is no other hope, no other way, I will do that; but not *till* then."

Mr. Rashleigh, who is a cunning, withered cinder of a man, with every spark of human sympathy burnt out of him in the great furnace of life, has hinted, as delicately as he can, that such a time is not far distant, if it be not already at hand.

It is all this worry, added to a thousandfold by his eldest daughter's misalliance, and his second daughter's poverty and oblivion, that makes the haughty, self-contained old man look so lined and furrowed to-day.

When the luncheon is over, and my lady has flitted airily away to perform her liquid tunings with the cut-glass bottle, Sir George retires to his own small, bare study, and sits down in the straight-backed arm-chair by the fire to think, for the thousandth time, over his position.

In the gathering twilight the room is nearly dark, save for the fitful glow of the coals, throwing strange, grotesque shadows upon the bare walls.

It is a dreary place, and a like reverie fills the old man's thoughts, shutting out all else. Looking back upon his life from that rigid old chair, what a dreary travel it has been! There is scarce one bright spot, one happy resting-place in all the journey. And yet it seems but yesterday that he was leaving college full of high hopes and high courage, thinking himself equal to Hamley (who was an honours man), if the examiners had only been impartial in their judgment. And then it almost makes him start to think that Hamley has been dead and gone these ten years! Ah, and so is Gabriel Brown, by-the-bye; and yes, and Harry Davoren, too, the gayest man in college; he can hear his laughter ringing still as he thinks of him! And what a host of others have left vacant places, now he comes to think of it!

Dreaming on thus, brings him in fancy to the day he wooed Elinor, and won her. Yes, in his way, he loved her. He recollects her the lightest partner in a valse, the pleasantest girl to take in to dinner, in all London. Good God, that she were only living now! His thoughts involuntarily turn, with a shudder, to that horrible personified lie that has just tripped away upstairs to drink brandy.

"If they can only patch up my affairs another five years, that will be long enough for me to have done with the whole thing," Sir George muses. "It's sad to have all one's old chums dropping off like this. To be sure, there's Curfew left, but he's getting senile with his twaddle about the girls of the Bermudas! I'd have him here if it weren't for that; he only makes me sadder, seeing the lusty, cheery fellow I remember, such a tottering, gouty old dolt! No. I have kept pretty much to myself through life, and I must fight it out alone at the end, I suppose."

With such sad attendant thoughts as these, Sir George falls into a half-sleep in his chair, whilst the fire blazes up brighter, throwing caricatures of the first Duke of Wellington, *en profile*, upon the wall.

Meanwhile my lady upstairs has had a free recourse to the cut-glass bottle with the straw-coloured contents, the effect being imperceptible, for there is an extremely worn and haggard look upon her face; but that always comes there when she is alone, and the necessity for acting absent.

A strange servant comes in to feed the fire, for Chipps is absent to-day on an errand: she is expected back every moment, though, apparently, for her ladyship asks the girl upon her knees before the grate, putting on coal silently piece by piece with her hands:

"Is Chipps returned yet?"

"No, my lady."

The replenishing done, the girl goes out with a noiseless tread, shutting the door so softly that my lady looks round to see that she is alone; satisfied on this point, she rises and moves to her dressing-table, pausing a moment before her glass thinking, with a sigh, how different the reflection used to be there! Then she takes a "Bradshaw" from a drawer, and returning to her seat, studies it long and closely.

"If she catches that train she should be here now" (looking at her watch). "And oh, what will her news be?"

Divested of its false simper, her face is terribly old and ugly in repose. At such times the marks of age she fences with so scientifically before the world appear to thrust home with a tenfold vigour, remorseless.

She has not judged the trains wrongly, for ere five minutes have elapsed Chipps enters the room, very quietly, with her wraps off, and no signs about her other than as if she had come from the next room.

There is no shamming between mistress and maid. The latter is in all the secrets of youthful artifice employed by the former. She comes straight up to her ladyship at once. There is no other greeting exchanged than an eager question by the mistress—a question asked with a breathless voice through parched lips:

"Did you find her?"

"Yes."

"Sit on that chair" (pointing to one beside the fire, and taking up a screen of delicate tracery and satin). "Now don't keep me a moment, or I shall scream. Was my surmise correct?"

"Yes," again, and only that one word.

My lady raises the screen between herself and her maid, so that her face is invisible. Speaking in that position she says, in a voice only a ghost of her own, feeble and quavering like the old woman that she is:

"Leave me alone, please."

Rising, and with a backward glance, half scorn, half pity, Chipps obeys. When she is at the door my lady calls her back:

"Paper and envelopes, and draw that table to me," she says.

With another backward glance, as before, only that scorn predominates now, Chipps goes out of the room.

Lady Kissingham sits a long time gazing into the fire listlessly.

"I wonder whether I did right to send *her*?" she muses, half aloud. "But that is done. What shall I do next? What will *she* do next?"

My lady draws the paper and pens to her irresolutely, finally abandoning the intention to write, rising and touching her bell.

Chipps glides in at once, silent as a spectre.

"Sit in that chair again." Chipps obeys, her fiery jet-black eyes shining so bright that one might almost imagine a smouldering fire hidden in her brain, and liable to flame out from them at any moment.

When they fall upon Lady Kissingham, her own invariably droop before them.

"Chipps, what do *you* say to this discovery?" asks the mistress. "What am I to do? Advise me, Chipps, for it is very awkward."

"Make all — and the only reparation in your power," replies the maid, with a hard, metallic voice.

"And that is, Chipps?" (with a ghastly attempt at gaiety).

"And that is to make a will in his favour."

My lady starts. "You are very dogmatic, Chipps," she says.

"I mean to be," is the dry answer.

"But I've already made a will—after my marriage —leaving everything to Sir George."

"Then make another."

"Suppose I'm wilful and won't, Chipps?"

The return of the forced air of gaiety is so horrible upon that haggard face in the firelight that even Chipps, catching sight of it, starts, and asks quickly: "Shall I light the lamps?"

"I would rather you didn't; answer my question, please—suppose I won't?" (with another ghastly attempt at gaiety).

"Sir George, I suppose, knows nothing of this?" is the questioning answer.

"Oh, Chipps, you don't—you can't mean—that you'll tell *him*?" (spoken, leaning forward, with all attempt at gaiety vanished, and only a horrible anxiety in its place).

"I *do* mean it."

"Oh, Chipps, think how kind I've been to you all along," whines my lady, half in tears. "Think what I've done for you since I took you off the stage!"

"What you've done for me!" cries the other woman, with a sneering voice. "Since Lord Netherby took *you* off the stage, you mean. Why did you take me with you into your grandeur—why?" She pauses as though expecting a reply; none comes, and she answers her own question. "Because I had the whip-hand of you. Because Lord Netherby never would have taken you unless I had kept silent. Is it not so?"

The question is put so suddenly and fiercely that my lady starts.

"Will you *never* forgive?" she asks in turn, with a trembling voice.

"Never! I swore it the day you stole my darling's heart from me. I swore it with tenfold determination the day you, by your conduct, drove him to his grave. You played me false throughout. You tried to hide from me that your child was *his* child, too. I found it out. Then, a third time, I swore never to forgive. Do you think I am a fool? Do you think my blasted life, lonely and disappointed, counts for nothing at all? I tell you it counts for a great deal. It shall make you, in spite of yourself, give reparation to your child by the man who loved me before you came between us."

The rage and bitterness of the woman are terrible to witness. My lady is a coward; she gives in at once before the storm she has raised.

"Tell me what to do, and I will do it," she says, in a faint voice.

"Write at once to your solicitor, and ask him to come to you here to take instructions for a fresh will."

"I suppose I must," sighing, and pulling the paper and pens towards her again.

"I shall stay here and take the letter to the post myself, or you will play me false again," says Chipps, fiercely.

"Dear, good Chipps, you shall see this new will, and witness it—there! Now go, please."

"Not till I have the letter."

My lady seems half inclined to make a fight of it, but alters her mind, and writes quickly as her trembling hands will allow her.

"There it is. Now go," she repeats, when it is done.

Taking the proffered letter, and with a backward glance of detestation, Chipps goes out. When the door closes on her, Lady Kissingham rocks herself back and forward in her chair, weeping tears that play sad havoc with the false youthful blush upon her cheeks.

Ten minutes later a message is brought to Sir George, startling him from his gloomy reveries:

"My lady has a headache, and will not dine tonight."

CHAPTER XIV.

"FOR THE CAUSE."

"I TELL you you were false throughout. If you can't intone better than you did yesterday, you had better give it up altogether," says Mrs. Saintly, speaking very loud and fiercely, and addressing her unlucky husband, who is sitting at breakfast on a certain Monday morning, Daisy not being down yet.

"I'm extremely sorry, my dear. I think I had a slight cold, and I forgot to take my usual glycerine lozenge before the service. I'm extremely sorry."

Mrs. Saintly is evidently ruffled this morning—though there is nothing unusual in the circumstance—sitting bolt upright and rigid.

The sore point comes out directly with her second cup of tea.

"I call it positively disgraceful! Lady Kissingham has, in reply to my third application, sent me only ten shillings for the mothers' meeting! A woman rolling in wealth—ten shillings! Scandalous!"

"My dear, you are warm," deprecates the Vicar.

"Warm! I *am* warm; I confess it. Ten shillings! Who ever heard of such a sum from the Manor?"

"Have you suggested the necessities of the case?"

"Of course I have—as much as I dared. I cannot offend the woman; that's what makes it so doubly annoying. If she stood a shade lower in the social scale, I could bully or cut her dead. But I can't behave so to Lady Kissingham. It would perhaps prevent her giving anything."

"I thought you particularly civil to her on Friday," says the Vicar, a bit reproachfully.

"Of course I was civil to her. Do you think me *quite* a fool? I tell you that's the bitterness of my position. I am compelled to be most civil to a woman I detest. Wives of clergymen—poor, unhappy things—always live in an atmosphere of being civil to women whom they detest—for the cause."

The Vicar sighs. He feels this home-thrust incontrovertible.

"Then there's a further reason for civility in this case, only you don't appear sharp enough to see it."

"What is that, my dear?" asks the Vicar, innocently.

"I thought not," exclaims his wife, with triumph. "I thought I should have to point out to you that Lord Maidenhair is constantly at the Manor now. Don't you see *why* he comes there?"

"I have always been under the impression, my dear, that he comes to endeavour to reconcile Sir George to his daughter Agnes's marriage with Cringleby."

Mrs. Saintly says nothing for an instant; she merely gives her spouse one of those domestic glances which wives *do* sometimes give their husbands when no one is by; glances which, translated into words, would, upon the authority of the New Testament, in ancient days have brought the giver of them in danger of the judgment.

The Vicar's eyes fall before this withering look to the contemplation of his eggs and bread-and-butter.

"Don't you see Maidenhair is much struck with Daisy?" asks the lady, scornfully.

"It never has struck me, I confess," replies Mr. Saintly, sadly. "But you have always said he is such a fool."

"And so he is—a terrible fool. But that doesn't matter when he is so rich. Think what a great thing it would be for Daisy!"

"Why, it certainly would, my dear, and he would subscribe, doubtless freely, to your charities."

"*Would* do so! Why, he has already done it. He has given me a five-pound note for application as I see fit."

"Dear me!" says the Vicar, much impressed. "Very generous indeed of him! What do you propose doing with it?"

"That I have not yet decided. Application as I see fit is such a wide discretion, you see. I have been thinking——" and the lady pauses.

"Yes, my dear, you have been thinking?"

"That I shall not be able to visit the poor much longer without a new ulster. I doubt whether, on the whole, it would not be more important that I should be able to visit the poor for their own sakes, than that the money should be applied directly to the various local charities."

"You don't mean, my dear, that you think of applying the money for your own raiment?" asks the Vicar, with as much horror as he dares in his voice.

"I *do* mean it. Is it not for THE CAUSE? Indirectly, I admit, but for THE CAUSE?"

This "for THE CAUSE" style of argument always collapses the Vicar. It does so now.

"You know best, of course, my dear," he says. "If—though even as you say indirectly—for THE CAUSE, you do right. I think perhaps you had better buy the garment."

Here the entrance of dear, rosy little Daisy, fresh as a bright-eyed summer morning, with a kiss for each of her parents, puts an end to the discussion.

"Dear Daisy," says her mother, fondly, "you must come with me to call at the Manor this afternoon. There is a great friend of yours staying there, you know."

Perhaps the one redeeming point in Mrs. Saintly's hard, worldly character, is her love for her child.

Daisy blushes—yes, positively blushes—as she replies, "Yes, mother dear, I'll go with pleasure;" and she really looks as though (for the only occasion in existence, perhaps) the two last much-abused words are spoken truly.

CHAPTER XV.

MILVERDALE VICARAGE AGAIN.

AS bright a summer's day as ever made the cattle stand lazily in the shade of trees, waging war upon tormenting flies with slow whiskings of the tail, and sleepy flappings of the ears, shines down in all its glory upon the little verandahed front of Milverdale Vicarage.

Under the verandah's shelter, with windows behind her open to the prettiest of Vicarage drawing-rooms, sits Agnes with her son upon her knee.

A little whispering breeze comes stealing round the angles of the house, and lifts, ever and anon, the curls about her brow, with touch soft as love's first kiss. So soft, that fluttering across the infant's face, it merely makes him turn a little in his sleep, and smile.

In front, the bold sweep of the landscape, hill and dale, lies in shadow and in sunshine—like the path of life. The happy face of Agnes turns at the sound of wheels coming up the little avenue from the white gates by the road; turns from the infant upon her lap to her husband driving home; turns with such a glance of greeting upon it, as would make many a lonely striver sigh for the like, could he see it.

But Robert Cringleby is not alone. There is a neatly-dressed, pleasant-faced young man along with him, with whom Agnes shakes hands warmly, and says:

"Oh, Lord Maidenhair! So you *did* catch the train after all. It *is* good of you to come here—and—what *do* you think of our boy?" holding up the little mite of humanity for inspection.

"Do you know I have been looking forward to this two days' visit here for ever so long," answers the guest. "It will be the greatest treat of the whole year to me, I am certain; and the boy is a splendid little fellow." He speaks as though he really means his words, and the friendship they convey.

Robert Cringleby returns from the stables, where he has seen the fat pony comfortably housed, and joins the group.

"I was only just in time for the train at Muddlebury," he says; "it was so tremendously hot that I hadn't heart to hurry my large steed."

"I should have walked on and met you, and enjoyed it," Maidenhair says, laughing, "though the sun is, as you say, hot. Why, Cringleby, where's your net? Fetch it at once! Look at that brimstone butterfly. I never saw a finer specimen!"

With a naturalist's ardour when in pursuit of game, the Vicar bolts into his study and out again with the hand-net with astonishing rapidity, but the peer is already in full cry half-way across the lawn, his hat in his hand, ready for a capture, and his whole energies directed to effect it. The host is not slow to follow, and within a couple of minutes the two are performing prodigies of activity among the flower-beds, with the enthusiasm of their school-days. Meanwhile, Agnes, happy Agnes, stands beneath the verandah's shelter, looking at them with a smile upon her face. A nursemaid comes and takes the infant indoors, and still she stands smiling at those two laughing men chasing the butterfly, which seems as difficult to secure as happiness.

They disappear behind a shrubbery now, and the little matron passes through the French windows into her tasteful little drawing-room, to busy herself with the spider-table and the tea-cups.

"Did you catch it?" when the sportsmen come in breathless from their chase.

"No, Mrs. Cringleby, it escaped us after all! Perhaps it means to give us another run, as the fox-hunters say, to-morrow."

Agnes laughs as she hands each his tea. "I can't say I'm sorry; it seems a bit cruel," she says.

When they are all sitting out again in the cool of the evening, the conversation turns upon the old life and the old neighbourhood.

"I was there last week," Maidenhair says, in reply to a question. "I was there to—to——" and he hesitates.

Husband and wife look at him in surprise. He sees the look and says:

"I'll tell Robert all about it to-night. This, though, I can say now—I did my best, as I always do, with Sir George; I fear hopelessly. Your father is very obstinate, Mrs. Cringleby."

"He is, indeed," Agnes says; and sighs.

"He has answered none of my letters, even the one I thought he would be sure to answer," the Vicar says.

There is silence for a few moments, broken by the guest.

"Lady Kissingham——"

The sudden tolling of the church bell, close by, makes them all start when he has got thus far.

"Robert?" Agnes says, inquiringly.

"Yes, my dear. I should have mentioned it, but it escaped me; poor widow Brown died this morning."

"Oh, Robert! Your first death since we have been here!"

No one speaks for a few moments, whilst the solemn tolling of the bell rolls out upon the cool evening air, telling of the end—or the beginning— who shall say which?

In a few moments, the Vicar says:

"You were saying——?"

Lord Maidenhair turns towards the speaker, and with the dreary accompaniment of the passing bell continues:

"I was saying — let me see. Oh, yes; I was saying that Lady Kissingham is looking very changed. I can't quite describe *how* changed; but not at all what she used to be. I noticed it the moment I saw her; indeed, I mentioned it to Sir George, but it had escaped him."

The tolling has ceased now, and a great white, flapping owl wheels above the lawn, uttering its unearthly cries. They all three sit watching it in silence, each deep in thought, a long time. The tinkle of a distant sheep-bell, the gentle lowing of unseen cattle at peace with all the world and obliged to mention it, are the only audible sounds.

"Is it not dreamy?" Agnes asks at length. "Our life here is a pleasant, endless dream. It seems hard to believe the world is full of life and bustle, plotting, scheming, striving, each against each, whilst all is so quiet here."

"There must be some dreamers in every world," Maidenhair says, softly.

The dreamy atmosphere and the dreamy talk has its effect, and another silence falls—longer than the first. So long, that it continues till the dew begins to rise, and a move is made indoors to supper.

That pleasant meal finished, the Vicar and Agnes begin singing favourite duets, to the great delight of the guest, who is strongly musical. The evening soon passes. It seems no time at all before Agnes is saying good-night, and stealing to print a farewell kiss upon her infant's sleeping face ere going to her room.

The two men, left alone together, first light their tobacco. With that most blessed of all our gifts in full combustion, the Vicar says:

"And now I am dying to hear what you could not tell before my wife. I thought you knew I have no secrets from her."

"I knew it perfectly. It was not that. I did not speak, because the matter was a personal one of my own. I preferred to tell you when we were alone, in the first instance."

"Well?"

"Do you recollect that afternoon in your rooms at Kissingham, over the beetles?"

"Yes, perfectly; you made me the happiest man alive by telling me that I might, you thought, hope for Agnes's love."

"Quite right; but did I not tell you something else?"

"Why, of course you did. You told me of your love for Elinor."

"That is why I did not like to speak before her sister just now."

"But you have surely got over that attachment by this time? Now, too, that she is married!"

"Yes, I have perfectly got over it—and—in fact, I am in love with some one else."

"I hope with happier results. Who is it?"

"Daisy Saintly; and she—returns it." He speaks with a great tremble of joy in his words.

"I congratulate you with all my heart," the Vicar says, extending a hand that is as freely met and wrung. "My best wish is that you may be as happy as we are here. I am assured you cannot be happier, for that were utterly impossible."

"Mrs. Saintly has been most kind," says poor, innocent Maidenhair. "She has consented to allow the marriage whenever we like to arrange it. I believe she is a thoroughly good woman, so interested in her parish. She is always importuning me for money for charities."

A smile rises to the Vicar's lips, but he suppresses it, and says:

"And when will the marriage be?"

"Two months hence, and we are going to travel —in Palestine, I think—Daisy wishes it." He speaks the word "Daisy" so proudly—as we used to speak some sacred name in days gone by.

There are few heartier hand-shakes given in this world of sham friendships and sham hearts, than these two men exchange at parting for the night.

CHAPTER XVI.

ON TWO HUNDRED POUNDS A YEAR.

TWO hundred pounds a year, manipulated with the most cunning skill, is not an income permitting or affording any great floridity of life on the part of the owner; when an "s" has to be added to the last word, still greater circumspection is required to perform that painful operation, known in the language of the crowd as making " both ends meet."

But, in spite of all this, there is the smartest of minute cottages standing under the shelter of the Sussex Downs where the income named produces most miraculous effects in happiness. This humble abode is that of Mr. and Mrs. Slingsby.

Ash Cottage, perched in a little nook back from the village street, is a kind of toy abode, perfect of the sort. There is a little toy carriage gate at one side, leading to a stable and coach-house almost small enough to be packed up and sent away in a Pantechnicon van. Within, a microscopic pony, of wonderful make and shape (groomed by the tiniest stable lad in all England), leads an exciting existence, his chief duty in the season being to draw Mr. and Mrs. Slingsby in a little toy cart, resplendent in varnish, over the Downs to catch such glimpses as may be of the harriers. This work, to judge by the way he steps and pulls, is thoroughly congenial work to him, and his pace on these occasions beyond all praise.

This pony and cart are the pride and joy of Mr. and Mrs. Slingsby, only purchased after deep cogitation and calculation. It happened in this way.

Elinor, upon their arrival at Ash Cottage, soon came to the conclusion that life would be the brighter for some sort of animal in the shape of horseflesh.

"It's no good, Tom," she said; "we shall never be able to afford a horse apiece, or even one between us. It must be a pony or nothing."

Tom assented readily, as he would have done gladly to any suggestion of his wife, and the sequel took the form of the equipage above described.

Perhaps Elinor was never prouder of her couple of hunters in days gone by, than she now is of Jack. Perhaps Tom never overlooked the personal comforts and "fitness" of any creature equine with the closeness and care he shows for this atom in the toy stable. Everything, though on the smallest scale possible to imagine, is perfect. From the bridle, which looks about fit to meet the requirements of a finely developed goat, to the cloth, stamped in the corner with two S's reversed, and about suitable for a greyhound, all is the very poetry of equipment. As to the cart, that might have come new yesterday from the Lowther Arcade.

Over the half-door of the loose-box, Elinor and her husband often lean amicably side by side gazing upon the wonderful steed that has all the love a child would have won had they been blessed with one.

Then, too, it is such a wonderful pony—drinking out of a tumbler, picking up pocket-handkerchiefs, and going through a whole host of interesting tricks.

Nor is this the only occupation of this strange couple—Mr. and Mrs. Slingsby. They often go for long, lung-opening "skelters" across the Downs, Elinor getting over the ground with that easy, swinging step of hers in a way that is delightful to witness.

"Why, this life is worth twenty years of the Kissingham one," she says to Tom, as they are walking homeward in the glow of an autumn evening, with a golden sun sinking into the blushing embrace of a crimson sky; "it's worth it to *me*, at any rate. What's it worth to you, Tom?"

Tom, looking at her, and seeing such a glorious rosy face with, oh! such wicked black eyes, can be easily excused a little exaggeration as he answers:

"What's it worth to *me*, Nell? Why, it's worth ten thousand years of the old life."

"You're a regular brick, Tom, and I believe you mean it," says Elinor, slipping a fondling hand through his arm. "I do believe you mean it."

He presses the arm through his, and they walk on thus in silence.

It is difficult to see, looking at the question comprehensively, that any other man with whom she might have married could have made such a woman as Elinor happier than she is. Sickened as she was by the overlying falsity, the tinsel of manner passing current for gold, of the curled and scented deceptions posing as men, with whom her former life was chiefly passed, this true, honest nature of Slingsby had such a charm for her as no other spell could weave. His very ruggedness had its value in her eyes. After a surfeit of French cookery we turn with gladness to the homely roast beef of old England. It would not have been so with nine out of ten women won by the good looks of their hunting groom. The majority, of course, would have tired long ago of their choice, and repented it. Fortunately for herself, Elinor is not one of these. She counted well the cost of the step she took, and she will never regret it.

It is a million chances to one, in this gnarled and distorted old world, that the two right people will never meet, or, meeting, understand that they *are* so met; but in the millionth case, no matter how incongruous the union—princess and peasant, king and beggar maid—it will be the happiest marriage the world has ever seen.

"Light the lantern, Tom; we must have a look at Jack before we go in," for it is quite dark when they get home.

Tom already has the matches in his hand. In his straw bed, with its plaited fringe, Jack looks round and puts a warm nose into the pocket of his mistress's ulster for the bread he so often finds there; nor is he disappointed.

As the two, husband and wife, stand there feeding their pet, and thoroughly intent upon the work, contented with each other and the world, it would require a vast amount of assurance upon the part of a spectator to talk about a misalliance.

Though the place is a stable, it should be borne in mind that there are heavier hearts, and ten thousand times blacker ones, in gilded drawing-rooms and embattled piles.

The voice alone is worth a great deal, in its affection and cheeriness, as Elinor says:

"Come along, Tom, old man, and I'll give you *such* a cup of tea."

CHAPTER XVII.

THE LENGTH OF THE TETHER.

SIR GEORGE KISSINGHAM, Baronet, sits, with the first-Duke-of-Wellington appearance marred by an expression of deep melancholy, in his uncompromising study, busy with accounts.

It is September, with gold upon the woods, and purple on the vine; the year has reached its zenith and passed it, weeping tears of faded verdure with every drift of the wind that sweeps hill and dale.

Sir George is not a brilliant accountant; besides, the accounts are unsatisfactory ones, ever showing balances against him. This may be the reason of his frequent pauses for thought.

Just at the moment he is wishing Rashleigh would come. Rashleigh *is* coming, the reason being that the time is close at hand when an effort must be made to lay that gaunt spectre, ruin, that has been haunting the Baronet so long.

"These solicitors always seem connected with what is unpleasant," Sir George muses, "and with situations that are uncomfortable!"

In his heart he feels that there must be something extremely wrong somewhere for a Kissingham to experience anything uncomfortable, and puts it down, vaguely, to the advancement and Radicalism of the age.

Then his mind wanders to the event of yesterday, the marriage of Maidenhair with Daisy Saintly; fools believing in such utter absurdity as "romance" and "love," and at this identical moment travelling post-haste for Palestine in a fairy-land of glamour. His own life has been nearly free from such nonsense as this, he thinks, remembering *his* loadstar has ever been position, and advancement, and importance. For an instant, and an instant only, a thought flashes light into his dark, worldly heart and asks: "Has it been worth all the fighting of your life? Has the dreary, empty, soulless existence been worth the price you have paid for it?" But such a flash to such a man is but a lightning one, darting out of sight and leaving greater darkness in its place. "Of course it has been worth it. Am I not a Kissingham?"

At this juncture Mr. Rashleigh is announced, and enters, bearing the black bag, which from its limpness invariably appears empty, peculiar to all solicitors for some unknown reason. Perhaps they carry their conscience thus; the emptiness we have mentioned gives no denial to this.

Mr. Rashleigh, as we have before stated, is a finely preserved legal cinder, dry as his own parchments, intensely professional, with excellent digestive faculties, given him by an agreeable Providence to atone for an utter absence of heart.

Placing the black bag upon a chair, when it instantly displays its vacuity by collapsing, Mr. Rashleigh advances with a little professional bow, and shakes hands.

"Pray find a seat," Sir George says. "*You* look well, Rashleigh; *you* never change or grow older."

"At least I don't rust out, Sir George."

When he speaks he has a way of snapping out his words, in a manner that seems to say: "Try *that*, and see how you like it."

In his heart he has a mingled feeling of contempt and admiration for his aristocratic client; contempt for his extravagant pride and follies, admiration for a certain power of endurance of the anxiety which has overshadowed him for so many years.

"Nor do I; but let us proceed with this painful business. Nothing fresh has occurred, I suppose?"

"Nothing favourable, Sir George."

"You said something in your letter," begins the Baronet, speaking with great slowness of utterance, "you said something in your letter about—a—a writ —I think you *called* it a writ?" (Rashleigh bows)— "about a writ being issued. Did I gather correctly that if you had not accepted service, I think is the term?" (Rashleigh bows again), "that writ would have been served upon me here?"

"Such would undoubtedly have been the case, Sir George."

The Baronet can scarcely believe his ears. That, even in this levelling age, a person should dream of the enormity of serving a writ upon a Kissingham of Kissingham, *at* Kissingham moreover, is almost beyond belief!

He is silent for some minutes, then he says:

"Now, I don't exactly grasp the effect of this legal form. What will be the result of this writ?"

"That Dewberry will sign judgment to-morrow, and, if the amount is not then paid, will proceed to place an execution in the house."

For once the stoicism of the old man is broken down. "Good God, Rashleigh!" he says, and bows his head upon his hands.

Mr. Rashleigh sits quite calmly, glancing with a piercing eye from his client to his black bag. Even *his* furtive brain can see but one way out of the difficulty, a way he has advocated a long time vainly.

"What is the amount of Dewberry's bill?" Sir George asks, presently, raising a wonderfully brave face to meet Rashleigh's.

"Thirteen hundred and thirty-five pounds, fourteen and sevenpence," answers the solicitor, with as many distinct snaps.

"There is no further way of raising money?"

"No further way. I am surprised I have been able to obtain as much as I have already borrowed for you."

"Then what *is* to be done?"

Mr. Rashleigh repeats in four distinct snaps the formula he has tried so frequently to force upon his client:

"Apply to my lady."

For the first time a wavering expression comes across the old man's face. The solicitor sees it, and takes advantage of it at once.

"Sir George," he says, leaning forward and speaking a trifle less harshly than usual, "Sir George, we have known each other a long time, long enough to remove any cause for garbled speech between us; therefore I ask you this one question: why did you marry Lady Netherby? We are old enough, Sir George, to omit all mention of love and such nonsense, and therefore I ask you, having a reason for so doing, why did you marry Lady Netherby?"

"It is an exceedingly painful question, Rashleigh; but I married her for—in plain English, for——"

"Diplomatic reasons, I take it," finishes the other, as the Baronet hesitates, as any man may well do at naming the horrible bare truth about such a transaction.

"Exactly, Rashleigh, for diplomatic reasons. You always put unpleasant things pleasantly."

Not heeding this doubtful compliment, the other goes on:

"Because you thought that a time might arrive when her—shall we say, influence?—would be useful to you and the house, the great and honourable house of Kissingham. Was it not so?"

A gesture of assent.

"Listen, Sir George," speaking slowly and impressively. "If ever there is to be a time when that influence is necessary, that time is NOW. If ever the Kissingham reputation and honour stood in jeopardy, that time is NOW. If ever you are going to receive some compensation for the matrimonial step you took a while ago, that time should be NOW—or never! I cannot put it more strongly to you than I wish to put it. Unless you apply to my lady, the honour of the house of Kissingham will be tarnished, I fear irredeemably."

On the only vulnerable point Rashleigh has attacked his client. Sir George visibly gives in.

"When should this appeal be made?" he asks, feebly.

"To-day—this moment. There is not a moment to lose. My lady may not keep large sums by her, and our need is immediate."

"It is a fearful position for a Kissingham," Sir George groans.

"Then you will apply to-day?" Rashleigh persists.

"Say to-morrow, Rashleigh—not to-day. Besides, my lady is not quite well at present. Would not a week hence do as well?"

"If you delay a week, you may as well leave it alone altogether."

The autumn evening has closed in, and the fire throws strange reflections of solicitor and client upon the bare, undecorated walls. There are candles upon the table, and by a movement Rashleigh asks, shall he light them?

"I prefer the darkness," Sir George answers. So they sit on silently in a gloom that deepens every moment, like the growing shadows across the old man's life. The battle fought out with himself is a fierce and bitter one. When he married Lady Netherby, there is no doubt Sir George felt, in a vague and indistinct way, that he was acting as became a Kissingham in allying himself with money; that marrying money advanced the honour and importance of his house; that the credit he would thus obtain would be sufficient to tide him easily over his few remaining years of life untroubled. It is probable he never imagined a day might arrive when he should be obliged to make an actual request for hard cash to his wife. A cold, proud nature such as his revolts against the bare thought of such a proceeding. If Lady Kissingham pre-deceased him, naturally he would inherit her property; but this would manifestly be a totally different matter. A very dark and unlooked-for day has dawned for Sir George, and he is a long time—much longer than a worse man would be—before he looks up to Rashleigh, and says, with evident effort:

"What must be, must be, I suppose. For the honour of the family name I am prepared to make this sacrifice of personal feeling and inclination. I will apply to Lady Kissingham to-morrow."

"You have made a wise decision, Sir George. I know a Kissingham never goes back from his word." The solicitor adds, by way of clinching the matter once and for all: "I shall go back to town to-night assured of the wisdom of the step you propose taking."

Declining all offers of hospitality, and carefully finding the black bag in the darkness of the room, Mr. Rashleigh goes out of his client's presence, as dry and crisp as a biscuit.

"These aristocrats have a certain something in their compositions which other people lack," he muses, travelling back to London. "Fancy a man half an hour deciding whether he should save himself from ruin because of a feeling of personal pride! Extraordinary greatness, or littleness, I scarcely know which!"

That night, at his dinner-table in Bloomsbury Square, when his son (as is the custom of youth) spouts Radicalism of deep dye, and wishes to know, really and truly, whether all men are not equal, Mr. Rashleigh annoys that young gentleman by firmly declaring his belief that "there is a certain *something*, Edward—there is a *something*," and refusing, though pressed, to be more explicit.

CHAPTER XVIII.

IN MY LADY'S ROOM

SIR GEORGE KISSINGHAM would dress for dinner and dine if he were going to be shot at nine p.m. Habit in this matter has become second nature to him, and to eat his evening meal otherwise than in a swallow-tailed coat and white tie would be utterly impossible to him. Kissinghams always *have* dressed for dinner since (as Elinor once said under irritation) they dressed the dinner itself in bygone centuries. Therefore, on this particular evening, Sir George sits, faultlessly costumed, abstractedly getting through a dinner of four courses and dessert. Abstractedly because he is wondering how my lady will receive his request on the morrow for pecuniary assistance. "I regret," the old man thinks, "that I am obliged to approach her when she is not quite well; but there is no help for it." And deciding upon the words he shall use, he proceeds with his meal.

It is quite true that my lady is not quite the thing. My lady has kept her bedroom the last five days with a cold caught through too liberal a display of the bony shoulders at a local dinner-party. My lady is much worse than she will allow. Upstairs in the girlish bedroom, where the tints are all complimentary, she lies upon a bed with a gauzy something of drapery deftly arranged around it. The lamps upon side tables throw a tinted light about the room through their delicately coloured shades; no footfall can be heard upon the luxurious carpet; all that wealth can do for comfort is there, and yet my lady tosses uneasily upon her bed. The fact of the matter is, my lady is very feverish to-night, and Chipps, watching grim as a spectre beside her mistress, reiterates the opinion that a doctor should be called in. Somehow Lady Kissingham has a rooted dislike of doctors. In a vague sort of way she feels they go behind the shadow of her deceptions and see her as she really is.

"Not a doctor, Chipps," she says, in a feeble voice; "to-morrow I shall be better."

But as time goes on, and the hands of the clock, that is a marvel emblematic love, point to nine, my lady, so far from being better, is decidedly worse. The liquid tunings, which have been freely resorted to during the preceding four or five days, have produced a very serious state of affairs. Chipps stirs the fire into a brighter blaze, as noiselessly as she can, and sits down in a chair beside it, bending her eyes upon the flames with her chin upon her hands and her elbows on her knees; she only takes her piercing gaze off the flaring coals to turn it towards the sufferer upon the bed. Whenever she does so turn it, there is always upon her face that strange expression, half scorn, half pity, that we saw there on her return from that mysterious Sunday quest in earlier days. She is wondering how ill that mass of falsity—every deception and artifice of which she knows—really is.

It seems my lady is dreaming, for low, half-spoken words reach the watcher by the fire. Chipps listens silently for some minutes, still gazing intently at the coals. Suddenly a word spoken by the dreamer makes her start and glance in that direction with a face from which every spark of pity has died out, leaving only a withering scorn and bitter hatred in its place. All unconscious of this, my lady repeats the word again, in a strange voice: "Willie!"

Rising quickly, Chipps, her whole face distorted by passion, glides to the bedside and grasps the speaker's wrist.

"Not *that* name!" she says, fiercely. "How dare you? Even in your sleep you shall not use it before *me*. If you were in mortal danger and your only hope lay in sleep, if you dreamed that word and spoke it, I would wake you though you died that instant. You base, false-hearted wretch! You shall speak that name in hell, but not on earth so long as I can help it!"

With a face horrible to see, she speaks in the suppressed tones of a rage too deep for noise, all the bitter fury of her disappointed life flaming from her eyes; never relaxing the grip upon the unresisting wrist, a grip that only wants the slightest variation of her anger to be transferred to the sleeper's throat.

Thus she stands, glaring upon the false woman who supplanted her years ago; the false woman who lies there before her, ghastly in painted cheeks and youthful artifices, both, for the moment, too horrible to picture or imagine outside the most fearful nightmare.

But the grasp upon her wrist does not wake my lady, albeit 'tis fierce enough, God knows. She wanders into other broken words. Stooping closer, still with a drawn, unnatural face, the watcher sees the truth. My lady is delirious.

Returning to the fireplace, Chipps rings the bell, and turning an ordinary face upon the maid who answers it, bids her tell Sir George that Lady Kissingham is very ill, and request his presence.

Sir George has finished his solitary dinner, and is reading *The Times* in the library when this summons reaches him.

"Say that I will come immediately," is the reply he sends upstairs, and finishes a leading article, with his gold-rimmed glasses clipping his ducal feature, and his head thrown very far back in his easy-chair to get a better light upon the print.

Lady Kissingham is still wandering when he enters her room; Chipps beside her, with difficulty hiding her feelings.

"Dear me, Chipps; really—is a messenger despatched for the doctor? This is very alarming," the old man says, coming up in his scrupulous evening costume to the bedside and looking down at his wife.

"Mary is at the door. I will tell her to despatch a groom at once," the woman answers, moving away.

For a few minutes husband and wife are alone together. Sir George stands in the same position still, noting the feverish tossings of the emaciated figure with the painted face.

Whilst he stands thus, Lady Kissingham repeats the name "Willie," distinctly, and then rambles off into incoherence.

"I did not know she had a brother—indeed, I am sure she has *not*, alive," the old man muses; "and Netherby's name was John. Strange! A random name, I should imagine," and he goes to the fireplace, and stands with his back to it, ruminating.

Chipps comes back and finds him thus.

"Do you apprehend danger?" the husband asks, with more anxiety than the maid can account for.

"I don't know—she is very ill."

"She repeated the name 'Willie,' whilst you were from the room. A random name, I take it, Chipps."

A spasm crosses the woman's face as he speaks, and she glances in a strange way from the speaker to the bed and back again, without answering. She is thinking how she could astonish that aristocratic old gentleman, if she chose.

Sir George Kissingham does not stay long upstairs. "I shall not retire to bed for some hours yet," he says, going; "send for me at once should you deem it necessary," and he goes back to *The Times* and the luxurious easy-chair before the blazing fire in the library.

Mr. Danvers, the local medical practitioner, lives some miles from Kissingham, and, though the groom despatched for him gallops his mount hard in a dreary moonlight, Chipps has a long and lonely vigil before the doctor comes; a dreary vigil in which all sorts of old memories flock into her mind and make her fierce and angry. Yet, when the sufferer turns and tosses she rises and stands looking at her now with a face that is not all hatred, for the thought has flashed upon her that *he* loved her—yes, false as she undoubtedly was, *he* loved her; and that unsatisfied, undying love she bears the man who first stirred her heart, makes her for an instant look upon her rival with a softening glance.

Dr. Danvers, a crisp, healthy-looking little man of middle age, takes a very serious view of my lady's illness. There is, he says, acute inflammation of the lungs, and consequent fever. He would like to see Sir George.

In the library Sir George receives him courteously. "I fear you have had a rough journey," he says, "but we thought the case urgent."

"The case is very urgent, Sir George. I do not wish for a moment to disguise from you that Lady Kissingham is in great danger. Indeed, as soon as the offices are open in the morning, I should wish to telegraph for a further opinion from London."

"This is very serious news, Danvers."

"It is indeed, Sir George. Lady Kissingham is no longer young; I entertain the gravest possible fear of the ultimate result."

"There is no immediate danger, I imagine?"

"No, not to-night. If friends are to be summoned it should be done in the morning. Her ladyship is quite ill enough to justify that proceeding, whatever the ultimate issue."

Sir George taxes his brain to think for whom he shall send, a process which results in one name only coming to him—Bingham.

"I can safely retire for the night, I suppose?" he says.

"Oh, certainly, by all means; I shall remain with her ladyship."

So the old man goes off to his night's rest, wondering what will be the outcome of this new state of affairs, and tosses uneasily through an unrestful night.

CHAPTER XIX.

LADY KISSINGHAM RECEIVES A VISITOR.

A GRAY-EYED morning looks into my lady's sick-room, and sees her worse than on the preceding night; sees Chipps, the stern and unforgiving, still watching beside the bed, with a white face and keen, devouring eyes; with Dr. Danvers fallen asleep in an easy-chair beside the fire that has burnt ashy and pale, too, like the watchers.

It would be difficult to tell from her face what emotions are uppermost in that gaunt woman's heart, as she stands gazing upon the wreck upon the bed. Hatred and love, so different, and yet so alike, so often inextricably mingled in an unfathomable mad passion, might both exist beneath that eager glance directed to the tossing sufferer.

Presently the doctor wakes with a slight start, and shaking himself as he rises, goes to the other side of the bed and places his hand upon the wrist lying inert upon the coverlet. After an instant thus, he raises his eyes from the patient's face and exchanges a glance, quick but expressive, with the maid.

He goes back to the fire and Chipps follows him. In answer to her questioning glance, he says, softly: "Sinking fast; despatch this message to London; it is half-past seven, the offices will be open," and sits at a spider-legged table to write the telegram.

When the message is sent off he stands at the foot of the bed looking at the uneasy slumber of my lady, who mutters in her half-unconscious sleep, Chipps meanwhile watching him eagerly.

"Sir George should be called, I think," he says, speaking low and with an elbow upon the bedstead foot; "and I should like to be shown into a bedroom where I can have a wash."

Chipps, quite silent, rings the bell and gives the necessary directions.

For the last time on earth the two women—bound together by such a strange, lifelong bond of union—are alone each with each.

The maid, passing to the bedside, takes one of the withered hands in a strong, nervous grasp, and regards the withered face intently. Something in the pressure of the hand rouses my lady, who half uncloses her eyes, and seeing the watcher, knows her.

"Chipps," she says, faintly, "Chipps."

"Yes."

"How bad am I?"

"Very bad indeed."

"Do I *look* so?"

"Yes."

A moment's pause for thought, and then, very feebly:

"A tinted curtain, Chipps—at the window."

"Is *that* all you have to say?" asks Chipps, with a rising fierceness in her voice; "*that* all, when you are in mortal danger? *That* all, at such a time, when it may be your last chance of telling me that you are sorry for that undying wrong you did me?"

But my lady has dozed off again, whispering incoherently of belladonna.

Half an hour later, Sir George, clean-shaved, prim, and starched, is standing looking at his wife, whilst the doctor is mixing something at a side table.

Chipps is still at her post, never raising her eyes from the face of her mistress.

The doctor, his mixing finished, comes again beside his patient and feels her pulse. There is something so unmistakable in the pallid face, that Sir George takes him aside and asks: "How long can it last?"

"I cannot say; it is all a matter of constitution. I do not think she will regain consciousness; there is absolutely no hope."

To do him justice, Sir George is deeply grieved. Although he has wired for Rashleigh, though he knows that his wife's death will end victoriously that wearying struggle he has waged so long with the grim spectre, Ruin, still he is sorry as he stands again beside the bed watching for the end.

The silence is profound for a long time, then my lady is heard muttering incoherent words. Sir George bends down to catch them. They only refer to dreams of by-gone vanities, and then turn to broken requests for a certain tarlatan ball gown she wore thirty years ago.

Sir George raises his head and sighs. Chipps the immovable looks on grimly.

Another silence, the doctor looking at his watch and calculating when the great man from London can arrive.

What is this? My lady is suddenly repeating whole sentences in a voice that is almost powerful.

Chipps knows what it means, and flings herself with a shriek upon the bed in a passion of tears. That mysterious power, the mind, working in cycles which ever bring the beginning and the end close together, is repeating portions of a part she played so long ago upon the stage.

Unintelligible to Sir George, unintelligible to the doctor, and interrupted by the hysteric sobs of Chipps, my lady wanders on through long sentences for a few moments, and then breaking off with a suddenness that makes the listeners start, asks in a coherent voice:

"Where is Tom Slingsby?"

Sir George looks at the doctor in speechless amazement. The doctor, scarcely less astonished, returns the look.

"Send for Tom Slingsby at once," cries her ladyship, half sitting up in bed and gazing anxiously upon the startled faces of the watchers. "I can't die— I won't die without his forgiveness, and yours, Chipps—yours. Do you forgive me—do you?"

She speaks in a voice of terrible entreaty, with an

anxiety fearful to witness, as she turns a ghastly face, that still bears traces of paint and powder, to her maid.

"Yes, yes, yes, I forgive you," says Chipps, eagerly, kneeling upon the bed and supporting the wasted figure that has assumed almost a sitting posture in its wild excitement. "Don't say another word—*I* never will—don't let them know *now*," she whispers in my lady's ear entreatingly, and then, turning to Sir George and the doctor, she goes on quickly: "She doesn't know what she says. Take no notice of it, poor, poor thing!"

It would seem that the dying woman hears the words, for she turns a bewildered but grateful face towards her supporter. A darting ray of sunshine flashes into the room, lighting up the strange group around the bed with a sudden brilliance. A calm spreads over Lady Kissingham's face—a calm that, as though by magic, smooths out all time's wrinkles there. Now she mutters a few broken words of some petty vanity, and so, with her head sinking slowly down to rest upon the shoulder of the woman whose life she has blighted, and with that woman's arm about her, my lady goes through the portal parting this world from the next, babbling of powder-puffs.

CHAPTER XX.

FACE TO FACE.

IT has been said that, on learning the serious nature of my lady's illness, Sir George telegraphed for his solicitor; he took that course because he knew time important, and that it was necessary to make certain arrangements, easy under the circumstances, to delay the proceedings of various eager and litigious creditors. This message was despatched immediately before going to the death-bed of his wife. No sooner had that death occurred than Chipps, scarcely yet recovered from the strange grief that overcame her at the end, despatched a telegraphic summons to her late mistress's solicitor, Mr. Poppenhoe, on her own account, without word to any one, requesting his presence, and telling of his client's death.

Therefore it chanced that Mr. Rashleigh and Mr. Poppenhoe, each in his respective offices, looking at "Bradshaw," naturally selected the only midday train stopping at Kissingham, and so travelled down together, by a singular coincidence, in the same compartment. Looking at his travelling companion, each (noting the black bag, apparently empty, which either carried) somehow guessed the profession of the other, and so fell to conversation. Thus, still deep in converse, they travelled in the same fly from the station to the Manor, only separating on the butler's message that Sir George wished to see Mr. Rashleigh immediately upon his arrival.

The Baronet is, as usual, in his bare little study, and thither Rashleigh goes to him.

"This is sad news, Rashleigh," the old man says, greeting the new-comer with a cold white hand.

Mr. Rashleigh—unfathomable as he usually is, admitting nothing, and denying nothing—to-day wears an unwonted gravity.

"It is indeed, Sir George," he says, taking the chair pointed out to him, after arranging for the safe placing of the black bag.

There is something in the tone of his voice, something in the glance that accompanies his words, that impresses his hearer with a vague, uneasy feeling he cannot define.

"It is unpleasant, at such a moment, to speak of business," the old man says, rather hurriedly; "but I take it, Rashleigh, that mine will not allow of delay. This sad event has, I imagine, smoothed out *our* difficulties, Rashleigh?"

Mr. Rashleigh does not speak for a few moments. He looks steadily at the meagre fire smouldering in the grate, as one in doubt how to convey best what he wishes to say. Then crossing his legs, and looking up, he says suddenly, with a piercing glance at his client:

"Are you aware that Mr. Poppenhoe, my lady's legal adviser, is in the house?"

"I was not. I did not send for him—who did?"

"My lady's maid, Chipps."

"A strange proceeding, Rashleigh!"

"Not under the circumstances, perhaps. I travelled down from town with him."

"Yes?"

The word is spoken in a tone of inquiry, for there is still in Rashleigh's manner a something that conveys the impression that there is more to follow.

The solicitor is silent again a while, taking no notice of the questioning tone. At length he says:

"Do you know anything of Lady Kissingham's past life?"

"I know what the world knows—that she was the late Lord Netherby's widow."

"Nothing more?"

"Save that she was wealthy—she *was* wealthy, Rashleigh?" asks Sir George, with sudden anxiety, for something in the lawyer's manner makes him fear some serious disclosure.

"She has left, I believe, about sixty thousand pounds."

Sir George sighs relief. Still the lawyer looks at him with a curious expression.

"I have learned to-day something of her ladyship's past; perhaps you would like to hear it?"

"It is really very immaterial, I imagine," says the old man, coldly. He does not like something in the tone of Rashleigh's remarks.

"Far from it; it is most important—to *you*."

"Then I had better hear it."

The words are spoken with resolution, and the Baronet's face backs them; though its owner knows he is about to hear what will be certainly unpleasant, it may be disastrous to him.

Mr. Rashleigh, thinking of that "something" he insists upon to his Radical son, and watching the old man closely, proceeds:

"I caution you, Sir George, that what I am about to say will shock you. Shall I proceed?"

"At once," without a shadow of hesitation.

"The late Lord Netherby, when at Brighton, met the lady in question under somewhat unusual circumstances—she was acting at the theatre there."

Rashleigh pauses. "Go on," says the old man, and he proceeds:

"He fell in love with her, and proposed at once. She accepted him. They went to London immediately, and were married."

"Yes?"

"She concealed from his lordship that at the time she was already married—that she had a son."

A spasm shoots across the old man's face, but he merely says "Go on" again.

"The child's father, on learning what she had done, committed suicide."

"And the child?"

"Still lives—to inherit his mother's wealth, for she has made a will leaving everything to him—Tom Slingsby."

Without word or movement, Sir George Kissingham sits staring straight before him.

Rashleigh, who has expected some outburst, gazes at him with amazement.

There is painful silence whilst the old man realises that he is ruined utterly. That he is worse than ruined—disgraced. Of course, his daughter—or, indeed, both of them—must know of this terrible scandal. Tom Slingsby, too, of all people in the whole world, *her* son! To a nature such as Sir George's the blow is crushing. What he suffers during that long pause it is impossible to imagine. It is as though some horrible nightmare were upon him, stopping his breath, whilst those two words thunder ceaselessly in his brain—"Tom Slingsby, Tom Slingsby"—on, on, on with a maniacal energy—"Tom Slingsby—*her* son and your groom! *This* is the woman whom you married"—and it means utter disgrace and ruin. He knows now why the horrible painted lie, which has only become a reality in death, uttered that name which he took to be the wandering of delirium. The last thoughts of a guilty mother, who had forsaken her child, going back to the blot upon her life, when that life was closing for ever! He sees the whole case clearly, and the horrible haunting name thunders louder than ever. But he must make an effort. Looking back upon it now, his whole life seems to have been but a vast dreary effort to hide the truth of his own heart from those about him. With all his faults he has a sort of desperate courage, which does not forsake him now.

He collects his faculties, though with evident effort.

"This means ruin, Rashleigh," he says, very quietly, in his old even tones. "I know that perfectly. But the immediate question is the present. All you have told me is known, I imagine, to yourself and Poppenhoe only?"

"With the exception of this maid, Chipps."

During that preceding painful silence it would seem that Sir George has arranged his plans, for he goes on decisively:

"Then you must see her, and also Poppenhoe. They must be kept silent till after the funeral, you understand? There must be no public scandal till *that* is over; afterwards, I must be left alone with the world to fight my own battle."

The solicitor is more than ever convinced of that subtle "something" now, for there is no trace of fear for the future or repining at the present in voice or manner of the old man who has played his last card and lost.

"So much I can doubtless arrange—but the future, Sir George? I sympathise deeply with you, I can assure you."

"It is good of you to say so, but I would rather you would not mention anything of the sort. Sympathy is extremely unpleasant to me, Rashleigh."

"Your daughter will be very rich. I have no doubt——," the other is beginning when Sir George cuts him short abruptly.

"Rashleigh, you forget; I *have* no daughters. They chose their own lives some time back, knowing the consequences of the course they took. Present circumstances in no way alter my determination as expressed then."

That mysterious "something" again! the solicitor thinks. A ruined man disowning a daughter with a fortune because he had sworn to do it in times past! He can hardly believe his ears.

"There is no time to be lost, I should think, Rashleigh," the old man says presently, still unmoved; "you had better see Chipps and Mr. Poppenhoe at once. If Poppenhoe proposes staying the night here, tell him I shall be glad to see him at dinner. Do you return to town to-night or remain here? Take whatever course you consider best."

Mr. Rashleigh, it seems, returns to London immediately; the invitation to Poppenhoe he will deliver.

"And add," says Sir George as the solicitor is leaving the room, "add, please, that I know everything, and do not wish the subject alluded to between us."

"Wonderful!" says Rashleigh, when he has left the old man alone. "Wonderful! He'll be as stiff, and civil, and mighty, as though he owned the county! There certainly is a something"

CHAPTER XXI.

AND LAST.

THROUGHOUT all those five long days intervening between Lady Kissingham's death and her burial, Sir George preserved outwardly his cold, polished, suave demeanour. What the agony of that period was to him will never be known. All through the autumn nights his pacing footfall could be heard traversing his bedroom, and his couch was scarcely ever pressed.

Mr. Rashleigh, who really took a sort of awed interest in the great wreck, paid constant visits, marvelling.

At the funeral, attended only by Sir George, the two solicitors, and Mr. Bingham, the old man was as cold and formal as ever in his life before. Several times has Rashleigh sounded him as to the future, and each time has he evaded the question with indifferent silence, or cold sarcasm.

The whole thing to Mr. Rashleigh is incomprehensible.

"How will he take the real crash when it comes?" he constantly asks himself. He has not long to wait for a reply.

Hydra-headed rumour, in spite of all precautions, has got abroad. A whispering breeze has told that there will shortly be a smash at Kissingham Manor. The news has spread to London, and the result is that the funeral party has not been an hour returned, before a certain official, with two attendants, arrives, and, in the presence of Mr. Rashleigh, informs Sir George (with apologies) that the attendants must remain until a certain sum is discharged.

Still the old man makes no sign. The official is informed that the two attendants will be made comfortable, and retires as much astonished as the solicitor.

"I don't know any details of your private money matters," the latter says to Sir George, before going back to London that night, "but if a few hundreds would be of any use——"

"I thank you, I have sufficient money to pay all the servants, and I require no more," is the cold rejoinder which greets perhaps the only case on record of a like offer from such a quarter.

When left alone, Sir George, ringing the bell, requests his astonished butler to bring all the wages books. These he pays, methodically, from a drawer in his writing-table, with a month's extra money, and an intimation that after a week he will not require their services. He knows the sale must take place that day week. So quietly, and in such ordinary manner is this done, that the butler afterwards declares that he saw nothing unusual in Sir George's look or manner at the time.

That day, and the following ones, the old man gives no hint of his plans for the future.

What his sufferings must be it is impossible to say. With men busy making out catalogues of the furniture, and affixing the lot-labels as they go; later, the day before the sale, a mixed multitude (chiefly dirty) thumping the chairs, and making personal remarks about the family portraits; through all this Sir George stays on in a silent, apparently half-dazed condition in his bare little study, where those who enter and see him, retire abruptly. All this (if he is thoroughly conscious of it) must be such an agony as few are called upon to endure.

The last day of all arrives at length. To-morrow the auctioneer will disperse those various family relics, once the pride of Sir George's heart.

It was remembered afterwards, that during the midday dinner-hour (the last meal the servants took in the house, for they all left that afternoon), the old man was seen wandering about gazing at the pictures, and apparently taking leave of each object endeared to him by long association. Towards five o'clock he was observed to take his hat and make his way by a footpath through the park to the churchyard, why, no one knew, though some say he stood uncovered for a long time in the twilight, by the grave of his first wife.

From the churchyard to the Vicarage is only a few paces, and thither Sir George proceeded and rang the bell. Mr. and Mrs. Saintly are at home, he is told, and shown into the drawing-room. But a change has (it appears) come over Mrs. Saintly. Mrs. Saintly's daughter has married a lord, and the good lady feels that under such important circumstances she is a very different person to the Vicar's wife who cringed before the Baronet in the past and craved subscriptions; besides, the Baronet himself is in hopeless difficulties. These two reasons combined make Mrs. Saintly endeavour to be grand—an endeavour made by maintaining a solemn silence, or only making some frigid remark.

"I came, Saintly," says Sir George, firmly, "because—from circumstances of which you are doubtless aware—I am going to leave you immediately. We have pulled together very fairly for a good many years. I don't like to—go—without saying good-bye."

There is no suspicion of a tremble in his voice as he extends his hand, which poor Saintly (with a fearful glance at his wife) seizes and shakes vigorously, as he mutters some pointless hope about "brighter days."

Such farewells must necessarily be sad ones—to all save Mrs. Saintly and such as she—and there is a decided moisture in the Vicar's eyes as he goes out to the door with Sir George, and watches his tall figure, once so upright, disappear in the wild, stormy evening.

"I am heartily sorry for him," he says, coming back to the snug fire over which his charming wife sits in awful majesty.

"He should have behaved more wisely," is her answer, spoken with the rigid propriety of one a trifle more than human.

"My dear, he has been very good to *us*."

"Well, it was only his duty to be so." Such is the logic of Mrs. Saintlys, all the world over. To recollect that to "err is human" is no palliation of a sin or a folly with them, though they can discount great actions by the score with their everlasting "only his, or her, duty" *formula*.

Sir George meanwhile has gone back to his bare little study, and sits there staring straight along a vista of misery at Ruin—the intangible spectre that has haunted him so long—intangible no longer.

The servants have all left. The occasional footfall of a broker's man in the empty corridors is the only sound audible. Even the untended fire has gone out, and the old man shivers as he sits there amid the ruins of his greatness—the last of the Kissinghams! He is only half conscious; the blow which he scarcely yet realises has stunned him. In the dark he turns towards the accustomed clock, a tall eight-day one in the corner. It has told the minute-beads in the great rosary of time since the day he remembers when, as a little boy, he was afraid of it; it has stopped now. The old man tries in the dark to tell the hour by his own watch; the figures are too small for his dimmed eyesight. With a sigh he gives up the endeavour, and begins groping in a drawer of the writing-table at which he sits, for something so iron and so cold that he shivers as his hand closes upon it.

Suddenly the door opens, and a voice he knows exclaims: "Why, father, you really are a most extraordinary person! All the servants gone; selling off the ancestors, I see they're all numbered! 'Kissinghams, ladies and gentlemen, remarkably old and dirty; who will start the bidding?' What *has* come to you?" Elinor walks about the room as she talks, searching for matches.

Sir George tries to speak; mingled feelings of rage and misery combined get in his throat and stop him. With a slight incoherent muttering in a strange voice, he slips gradually off his chair on to the floor, and lies at his daughter's feet, insensible.

"Confound the matches! And where *is* Tom?" cries that young lady, with irritation. "And I never knew the guv'nor go in for fainting before. *Tom!*"

Tom (with a broker's man) is speedily in attendance, and the old man is carried to his sadly disarranged bedroom. Tom (who is suffering from a bad attack of daze himself consequent on the surprises of the last few days) is despatched for the doctor, whilst Elinor does all she knows for the still insensible figure on the bed.

"Everything in a muddle since I was here last," she says to herself, energetically rearranging the furniture in its old order as she speaks. "And what has become of his old pride, to be selling off like this? He really *can't* have been upset about the death of her ladyship." The idea seems so droll that Elinor is obliged to stop, in spite of her father's condition, and smile. "He needn't have been so wild with me for marrying the son when he went in for the mother himself," she soliloquises, going on with her orderly work again. "If he were his old self I'd tell him so; but it won't do now."

She goes and bends her rosy face, that is so full of life and ever-varying expression, over the pallid one lying unconscious. A strange couple to be related as they are related; and yet by the light of the lamp she holds is traceable a shifting, unlike-likeness each to each.

"Now, Tom, go and see the auctioneer, and stop the sale at once," his wife tells her husband, when he has returned with the doctor. "Don't forget you can do any mortal thing you like now. Money will do anything."

She has been instilling this precept for the last two or three days; for, if truth must be told, Tom Slingsby has not risen to circumstances as quickly as might be. Without Elinor, it is probable he would never rise to them at all.

For a long time, Sir George Kissingham lay balancing, like scales, between life and death. But with the summer time he began to revive in earnest. Early in May he was able to sit in a chair at his open bedroom window, with all the blossom incense of early summer drifting in upon him to woo him back. Back to what? Not to his old self. The devoted nursing of both his daughters — for little Agnes has been at the Manor, taking her share of the responsibility—has saved his life; but the shock and its effects will be with Sir George Kissingham to his grave. Even Elinor — strong, practical Elinor —has felt her eyes fill with tears as she has sat beside him, listening to his childish talk that is so utterly unlike himself.

Mr. Rashleigh has come down frequently, and had long interviews with the doctor and with Elinor, and has explained the hopeless state of the old man's affairs.

Fortunately, in his present condition, one place is as good as another to him; and therefore, it is arranged at last that he shall go to Milverdale with Agnes.

The Manor is to let, and the old familiar furniture to be sent down to the house the Slingsbys have purchased in Sussex—all but the tall clock in the study, about which Sir George has so constantly inquired, that it is moved up to his room; there, though something of his childish awe of it has returned, he sits watching it for hours together, as he did all those long, weary years ago.

That clock will go down to Milverdale Vicarage with him, and will there record his hours till the day when, for him, such record shall be unnecessary.

There are many faces, mostly happy ones, crowding round our desk to say farewell—the fancy faces of our story.

Mr. Rashleigh is here waving a crisp adieu, and going back to Bloomsbury, more assured than ever that in the composition of the aristocracy "there is a *something*."

Elinor and Tom are here too, arm-in-arm, come up specially for our purpose from that large, rambling white house placed amid the hills and dales of laughing Sussex; that large white house noted throughout the county for its choice horseflesh, and where the stables are *not* the most uncomfortable part.

Why, this is Chipps! Chipps the austere, stealing wonderfully soft glances, unseen, at Tom Slingsby. With those savings she has collected through life, she lives in a trim little cottage hard by the Slingsbys' abode, happier than might have been expected.

There are some faces with us to-night that we cut dead, and refuse to see—Mrs. Saintly, for instance, and Mrs. Bingham, at whom we only look askance. But we give a farewell smile to the Vicar, and wish him a little more intelligence at parting.

There are some absentees. Maidenhair and his wife are still abroad, travelling through Palestine, and believing they must have discovered Eden in their happiness.

And Agnes—dear little soft-eyed Agnes! She is not here, because her household duties have prevented it. But lo! we wave our magic wand, and we are looking into the cosy little sitting-room of Milverdale Vicarage. There is Agnes, busy with some sewing, but ever and anon looking up with a smile to her husband.

Robert is sitting opposite to her, beside the fire, pretending to read (their *two* children—the one at the beginning, and the other at the end of life's journey—are both in bed), but half his time Robert's eyes wander beyond the edges of his book to rest lovingly upon his wife. So they will do lifelong. Whether wandering through flower-sprinkled fields in spring and summer, trudging stoutly between golden woods in autumn, by the blazing coals as now, at the year's close—ever that look in Robert Cringleby's eyes when they rest on Agnes.

What better ending of our story than to wish as fond a husband, or as fond a wife, to every reader of this page? May each winning such treasure, prize it as it *should* be prized; laying it close to the heart for ever, folding it closer with each year that speeds, resting loving eyes on that, and that alone, when all else is fading in that last darkness which precedes THE DAWN.

THE END

LONDON: SPENCER BLACKETT, ST. BRIDE STREET, E.C.

ONE SHILLING NOVELS.

BLACKETT'S SELECT SHILLING NOVELS BY POPULAR AUTHORS.

Price, paper cover, 1s. Postage, 2d.

99, Dark Street. By F. W. ROBINSON.

"Who loves a good mystery persuasively handled and sustained should be gratified by Mr. Robinson's '99, Dark Street.'"—*Saturday Review.*

Price, paper cover, 1s. Postage, 2d.

A Wicked Girl. By MARY CECIL HAY.

"The story has an ingeniously carried out plot. Miss Hay is a graceful writer, and her pathos is genuine."—*Morning Post.*

Price, paper cover, 1s. Postage, 2d.

Gabriel Allen, M.P. By G. A. HENTY.

Price, paper cover, 1s. Postage, 2d.

The Argonauts of North Liberty. By BRET HARTE.

Price, paper cover, 1s. Postage, 2d.

The Abbey Murder. By JOSEPH HATTON.

Price, paper cover, 1s. Postage, 2d.

A Mere Child. By Mrs. WALFORD.

Price, paper covers, 1s. Postage 2d.

Love Until Death. By R. WHELAN BOYLE.

Price, paper covers, 1s. Postage 2d.

The Queen's Token. By MRS. CASHEL HOEY.

*** This Series will be exclusively reserved to the works of well-known Authors. Other volumes are in course of preparation, and will be published at short intervals.

London:
SPENCER BLACKETT, *Successor to* J. & R. MAXWELL,
MILTON HOUSE, ST. BRIDE STREET, LUDGATE CIRCUS, E.C.

spinall's
Enamel

Sold
Everywhere

RKS: LONDON, S